Outer Banks
Pocket Companion

Insiders' Publishing
105 Budleigh St.
P.O. Box 2057
Manteo, NC 27954
(252) 473-6100
www.insiders.com

Sales and Marketing:
Falcon Publishing, Inc.
P.O. Box 1718
Helena, MT 59624
(800) 582-2665
www.falconguide.com

•

1st EDITION
1st printing

ISBN 1-57380-099-6

Introduction

Welcome to the Outer Banks — land of beginnings! You've landed in the same area where the first English colonists set up camp, Blackbeard and his band of buccaneers anchored and plundered along the shallow sounds, and Wilbur and Orville Wright flew the world's first airplane.

You have no doubt noticed that our fascinating stretch of barrier islands is virtually bursting with interesting things to do, places to visit and fantastic, widely varied culinary options and late-night haunts. In fact, there's no way that our ribbons of shifting sand can be fully explored in a day, a week or even a month filled with wall-to-wall activity.

So how do discriminating visitors decide what recreational pursuits are worth their while, which attractions are must-sees, where to go for the perfect dinner or after-hours ambiance?

You've got the answer right in your hands. The *Outer Banks Pocket Companion* will help you navigate these beautiful shores by providing all the information you'll need on area restaurants, nightlife, recreation, watersports and fishing. Hundreds of listings, compiled and composed by local Insiders who are experts on the area, are jam-packed into this handy, reader-friendly guide. It's your personal ticket to a glorious getaway.

So whether you're looking for a down-home dinner featuring locally harvested seafood, or four-star finery in our classiest restaurants; a night of dancing in a hopping club with live music, or just a couple of beers in a laid-back beach bar; wet and wild fun on a personal watercraft, or an educational afternoon spent exploring museums and lighthouses; an offshore charter to put you in the heart of the East Coast's best fishing, or just an hour with the kids on one of our local piers, let us help you make the most of your time with us.

So what are you waiting for! The best of the Outer Banks is ready to be explored in the *Outer Banks Pocket Companion*.

Table of Contents

HOWARD'S PUB
& Raw Bar Restaurant

AAA Approved

Serving 11:00 AM
till 2:00 AM Daily

928-4441
Ocracoke Island

*Over 200
Domestic &
Imported Beers,
Microbrews
& Wines*

Ocracoke's only ocean view deck

Screened Porch with Rocking Chairs

HOME
OF THE
OCRACOKE
OYSTER
SHOOTER

**Fresh, local
shrimp,
clams,
oysters &
mussels**

Kid Friendly

**Burgers, Subs,
Salads,
Pizza...
and more!**

Live
Entertainment
and
Big Screen TVs

Open 365 1/4 Days a year (Based on 4 year average)

Restaurants

Like critters from their winter dens, restaurateurs emerge en masse from their cold-weather haunts around March and return to work just about the time those wicked northeasters are no longer a threat. It's a busy time on the Outer Banks, with owners unshuttering buildings, sprucing interiors, hiring staff and tweaking menus. The restaurant business on these barrier beaches ebbs and flows according to the weather, and everyone knows it's life or death, business-wise, in the summer. People who run eateries aim to please — and mostly, they do. Whether you're treating yourself to a delectable dinner while on vacation or just trying to find a quick, satisfying supper for your hungry family after a long day on the beach, you'll likely find what you want and need on the Outer Banks. Dining out is one of the most enjoyable activities you can do frequently, easily and oftentimes, inexpensively. The Outer Banks has a wide array of restaurants from which to choose, offering food to please every palate and price ranges to suit any pocketbook. There are upscale cafes with European ambiance and unusual culinary creations and down-home fish houses where your meal may be caught only a few feet from your table.

International fare, as well, has made its way to these isolated islands with Mexican, Thai, Italian, Chinese, French and even Caribbean-style eateries springing from the sand in recent years. Ethnic cooking also has crept into even the most traditional restaurants, and many chefs have revised their menus for the summer season to reflect a wider variety of healthful alternatives and even vegetarian offerings.

Competition keeps increasing too. Besides the dozen or more restaurants that changed owners or managers over the winter, every year several more open in time for the summer season.

Increasingly, restaurants are opening earlier in the spring and staying open longer into the fall each year. The shoulder seasons have become popular times to dine out because the off-season offers the same friendly service and great food with less crowds. Most eateries now open by March and don't close their kitchens

until after Thanksgiving. Many even have decided to serve their full line of selections year round.

Although seafood has always been a mainstay for barrier island cooks and their customers, chefs schooled at culinary institutes around the world are making their way into Outer Banks restaurants and are changing the way we all eat out. Besides the traditional fried flounder, steamed shrimp and you-pick-'em blue crabs, which will never be removed from many area menus, bistros now serve poached salmon over beds of just-made saffron linguine; cafes coddle discriminating diners with everything from roasted duck breasts drizzled with raspberry cassias sauce to chick pea and black bean hummus dip with pita chips; and many eateries pride themselves as much on the food's artistic presentation as on serving the freshest, highest quality ingredients available.

Wine, too, is rapidly becoming one of our restaurants' biggest drawing cards. Several Outer Banks eateries host wine-tasting weekends in the off-season, and many have decided to serve 12 or more types of wine by the glass for those who want to sample several kinds. Wine-by-the-bottle lists expand each season, and restaurants along the northern beaches sometimes offer 50 or more varieties of the world's finest wines.

Most Outer Banks restaurants serve beer and wine, at least for dinner; however, those in Corolla and on Colington, Roanoke, Hatteras and Ocracoke islands are forbidden by law to offer mixed drinks. Some establishments allow brown bagging, however, whereby you can bring in your own liquor. Call ahead to make sure it's OK. And ask if they provide setups.

Dinner isn't the only meal to eat out, of course. A variety of bakeries, diners and even seafood restaurants now serve big breakfasts and weekend brunches. Most places are open for lunch throughout the summer, and some even serve bathing suit-clad customers just off the beach. The majority of restaurants, however, still require you to wear shirts and shoes. Many cooks will package any meal to go, though, and some eateries even have started delivering, with menus offering much more than just pizza that can be dropped off at your door.

If you're eating an evening meal out, feel free to dress as comfortably as you desire. Even most of the expensive, elite establishments welcome sun dresses, sandals and shorts. Some restaurant managers say everything from evening gowns and suits to jeans and T-shirts are acceptable at their linen-cloaked tables.

Reservations aren't taken at many restaurants. Others, however, suggest or even require them. The Blue Point in Duck, Ocean Boulevard in Kitty Hawk and Colington Cafe on Colington Island all get so booked up in the summer that you usually have to call at least three days ahead to secure a table. The fare at these fabulous places, however, is well worth the wait.

If sticking to a budget is a concern, you can have homestyle meals from tuna steaks to North Carolina barbecue for less than $8 in many Outer Banks family-style restaurants. Western Sizzlin', Golden Corral and, of course, fast-food eateries from McDonald's to Wendy's all also offer their standard fare here. For this chapter, we haven't included any chain restaurants; we think you already know what to expect from those spots.

Seafood is, and probably always will be, one of the biggest draws for Outer Banks diners. Caught in the sounds, inshore ocean and as far out as the Gulf Stream by local watermen, much of the

Price Code

For your convenience, we've included a pricing guide with each restaurant listing to give you a general idea of what to expect when the tab comes. The costs are based on entrees for two people, excluding appetizers, dessert or alcoholic beverages. Many area eateries also have senior-citizen discounts and children's menus to help families cut costs. Most entrees include at least one vegetable or salad and some type of bread. Prices vary, obviously, if you select the most or least expensive items on the menu; this guide is a generalization hitting the mid-range prices of restaurants' most popular meals. Here's our breakdown:

$	$25 and lower
$$	$25 to $45
$$$	$45 to $75
$$$$	$75 and higher

Price ranges do not reflect North Carolina's 6 percent sales tax or the gratuity, which should be 15 percent to 20 percent for good service. Some restaurants offer early evening dining discounts to encourage patrons to avoid peak dining hours. Most have at least two or three daily specials that change depending on the availability of food and the whims of the chef.

fish served here lived or swam near the barrier islands and often makes it to your plate less than two days after being landed. Some restaurants, however, are importing increasingly more fish from foreign countries. Ask your waiter where the seafood came from if you're fishing for Outer Banks-only food. If you want someone else to clean and cook your catch, Nags Head Pier Restaurant will gladly prepare your own "fish of the day" for you.

Raw bars always are great bets for relatively cheap, yet succulent, seafood. Oysters, clams, crab legs and shrimp are served on the shell or slightly steamed, and some places even include vegetables. Soft-shell crabs also are an Outer Banks speciality worth raving about, served from Easter through early July. Don't be put off by the spidery legs hanging off these crustaceans. Just consume the entire creature, shell and all — it's a whole lot quicker and easier than having to pick the meat out of hard shells once the crabs stop molting later in the summer.

If you're into picking your own crabs, however, you'll probably want to spread out some newspaper at your cottage or find an outdoor picnic table to absorb the mess. You can buy the locally caught blue crabs already steamed, or you can cook them yourself in a big kettle. You can catch your own crabs in area sounds, inlets and bays by dangling a chicken neck from a long string and letting the shellfish wrap its claws around the meat. Just be careful when you're taking it off the line to drop it in your bucket before it latches onto your finger. Always steam crabs while they're still alive, and don't eat the gray lungs or yellow mustard-like substance inside.

Restaurants in this chapter are arranged from north to south from Corolla through Ocracoke. Seasons and days of the week each place is open are included with each profile. Unless otherwise noted, these eateries accept at least MasterCard and Visa, and many accept other major credit cards as well.

We've also added some primarily carry-out and outdoor dining establishments that offer quick, cheap eats, cool ice-cream concoctions and perfect items to pack for a picnic or offshore fishing excursion.

Whatever you're hungering for, you'll find it here.

Corolla

Corolla Pizza & Deli
$ • Austin Complex, N.C. Hwy. 12, Corolla • (252) 453-8592

This take-out-only deli serves subs, sandwiches, Philly cheese steaks and pizza by the pie or slice for lunch and dinner. Each pizza is made to order on hand-tossed dough. Regular red sauce and gourmet white pizzas, including the ever-popular chicken pesto pizza, are available. During the summer season, Corolla Pizza offers free delivery. You can walk in or call ahead to have your order waiting. Corolla Pizza is open seven days a week in summer. Call for off-season hours.

Nicoletta's Italian Cafe
$$$ • Corolla Light Village Shops, N.C. Hwy. 12, Corolla • (252) 453-4004

Since this small Italian cafe opened six years ago near the red brick Currituck Lighthouse, it has earned a fine reputation for a wide variety of well-prepared foods. This classy little bistro features tables covered in white linen and each adorned with a single, long-stemmed red rose. Waiters whisk about in crisp black and white uniforms. A thick burgundy floral carpet cushions their steps, while Frank Sinatra tunes often echo softly in the background.

Nicoletta's menu features a variety of fresh seafood, veal, chicken, pastas and salads. Special appetizers and dinner selections change each evening, and there's an abundance of authentic Italian dishes from which to choose, all with wonderful homemade sauces that seduce the palate.

A select wine list is available, and homemade desserts change weekly. A cup of espresso or cappuccino is a great way to end the evening. Reservations are highly recommended; a separate room is available for private parties. Dress is casual, and children are welcome (there's even a special menu to suit younger appetites). Nicoletta's is open seven days a week in summer. Call for off-season schedules.

Horseshoe Cafe
$$ • Corolla Light Village Shops, N.C. Hwy. 12, Corolla • (252) 453-8463

Six years ago, Horseshoe Cafe brought Southwestern cuisine to the northern Outer Banks. Here you'll find homemade crab cakes seasoned lightly with chili powder for that Tex-Mex flair. Vegetarian chili also is a stand-out. There's also plenty of good seafood, steaks, chicken and barbecue on the menu. All the desserts are home-made, from Key lime pie to sopapillas drizzled with honey. Choose from a variety of flavored coffee, mocha cappuccino and even hazelnut espresso to top off your meal.

The decor here fits the theme. Bull horns, wool rugs, cacti and, of course, horseshoes line the walls. A Mexican tile bar offers a cool place to sit a spell and sip one of 25 kinds of beer served. The wine list is extensive too.

Horseshoe Cafe serves breakfast, lunch and dinner seven days a week in summer. Sandwiches are available for a light supper along with the full entree offerings. A children's menu offers smaller portions and prices, and the wait staff even provides crayons to keep your tykes entertained. Reservations are suggested.

Miriam's
$$ • Monteray Plaza, N.C. Hwy. 12, Corolla • (252) 453-2571

Owner/chef Ann Runnels has had a great response since she opened this New American cuisine restaurant in July 1996. Diners love Miriam's comfortable and casual ambiance with contemporary geometric decor and classy white walls, but people keep coming back for the creative cooking. Talk about mouthwatering: Try the seafood Napoleon, with layers of shrimp, scallops, crab, smoked salmon and puff pastry, finished with a roasted red pepper cream coulis. Or how about brown sugar and mustard-marinated sliced pork? It's sliced pork tenderloin served with braised red cabbage slaw and cheddar-scallion mashed potatoes. A different pasta dish is available every night, and one or two specials are offered daily. The specials are usually centered around the freshest fish available that day. Filet mignon, chicken and seafood dishes can also be selected off Miriam's delectable menu items.

A children's menu is available. There's also a full beer and wine menu. Make sure you save room for one of their desserts, which are all made in-house and are as fresh and sinful as you could ask for. Try the warm apple and blueberry oatmeal-crusted cobbler with whipped cream. Our other favorites include warm chocolate mint cake with raspberry sauce and bananas Foster cooked in brown sugar and rum, encased in phyllo dough. Miriam's is a nonsmoking restaurant open daily for dinner only May though December. Reservations are encouraged.

Sorrel Pacific Cuisine
$$ • TimBuck II, N.C. Hwy. 12, Corolla • (252) 453-6979

The only eatery in Corolla with a soundside view, this lovely restaurant with the lovely name offers fresh seafood and continental and American fare with an exotic twist. Sorrel is both an herb and the name used to describe a chestnut-colored horse with white markings — perhaps like one of Corolla's famous wild horses. Pacific cuisine, of course, is food that is flavored with Hawaiian, Chinese, Thai or Japanese spices. The decor — a blend of green, black and blue colors and Japanese rice paper screens shown off by lots of big windows — is cozy and doesn't overdo the Pacific theme.

For lunch, standard fare such as burgers, fish or shrimp-salad sandwiches are often served with a side dish of pineapple tossed with mango and coconut. Dinner offerings at Sorrel Pacific include such entrees as coconut-flavored shrimp, steak with roasted vegetables and mashed potatoes, tuna sushi rolled with rice and seaweed and fresh spring rolls. Fresh fish is prepared with delightful and palate-surprising Pacific flavorings. Vegetarian fare is also available, and there is a children's menu. Diners can choose a beverage from an extensive list of domestic and imported beers and wines. Specialty frozen drinks made with wine and all natural ingredients are very popular here.

Enjoy a drink in the enclosed windowed bar overlooking the sound, or sit outside on the patio for your meal or just a refreshing drink. Steamed shrimp and steamed crab legs are available at the bar.

As it embarks on its fourth season, Sorrel Pacific Cuisine is offering extended brunch hours in the summer. Call for the schedule. Brunch, which is mostly standard American cuisine, is available Sunday from 10 AM to 2:30 PM. In the off-season, only dinner is served. In the summer, dinner is available nightly, and lunch will be offered on varying days. Sorrel Pacific closes for a few months in the winter, so call for off-season hours.

Steamer's Restaurant & Raw Bar
$$ • TimBuck II, N.C. Hwy. 12, Corolla • (252) 453-3344

This 50-seat restaurant and raw bar serves lunch and dinner year round. Lobster, shrimp, oysters, clams and mussels are available as well as lamb, veal, grilled beef, chicken and even sandwiches. Diners will enjoy the waterside view from this upscale but casual restaurant that boasts 28-foot vaulted ceilings. If you have to wait for a table, you can wear a "patron pager" and stroll through TimBuck II until you're beeped. Steamer's also offers desserts and appetizers as well as microbrewery beers, wine and Black and Tans (that hearty, layered combination of Guinness and Bass Ale) to complement the fresh, local seafood.

Steamer's Shellfish To Go

$ • TimBuck II, N.C. Hwy. 12, Corolla • (252) 453-3305

The most innovative idea to hit the beach in a long time, Steamer's Shellfish To Go is Corolla's version of the popular New England-style clam bake. Housed in a separate location next to Steamer's restaurant, it's a gourmet seafood market that offers full take-out of

Photo: Courtesy of J. Aaron Trotman

Diners can choose from an abundance of eateries serving delectable dishes and offering impressive wine lists.

the best the Outer Banks has to offer presented in a refreshingly different fashion. Steamer's bills it as a service that provides the perfect night in. Steamer's Shellfish To Go features a full steam bar, gourmet dinner entrees to go and an extensive selection of wines and microbrews. Choose a mix-and-match pick of six of the microbrews to take home. Fresh local fish is also prepared for take-out. Or — here's the real fun part — your selection can be packed in its own steamer pot with fresh vegetables and taken home to steam yourself. The steamer pots are cans that contain layers of seafood, Red Bliss potatoes, onions and corn. You go home, add a cup of water and place it on your stove to cook. Thirty-five minutes later — presto! — you have a gourmet meal. Other offerings include soups, salads, seafood pasta salad, ribs, rib-eyes, side orders of fettuccine Alfredo and fresh Gulf Stream fish and plenty more. Shellfish To Go is open seasonally from 11 AM to 9 PM.

Duck

Sanderling Inn Restaurant
$$$ • N.C. Hwy. 12, Sanderling • (252) 449-0654

The restored lifesaving station at the Sanderling Resort just north of Duck houses one of the Outer Banks' most acclaimed restaurants. Multiple dining rooms enhanced with rich woods and brass offer peeks at the glistening sound through expansive windows. Here, progressive Southern regional cuisine is served for breakfast, lunch and dinner. A three-course, $15.95 Sunday brunch, available from 11:45 AM to 1:30 PM, is the best on the beach.

Start the morning off with Chef Glen Aurand's delectable menu, which has included malted Belgian waffles with fried apples and warm maple syrup or orange cinnamon French toast. For lunch, try such delicacies as the grilled fish of the day or a seafood platter featuring mussels, clams and shrimp. Other mouthwatering offerings include the oyster Po' Boy sandwich, cold poached salmon or classic shrimp. In the interest of serving only the freshest food, the menu changes frequently according to the season.

Dinner entrees include baked salmon Rockefeller, stuffed with spinach and oysters, and crab cakes made with all backfin meat. Seasonal, regional seafood is the menu's main focus, but beef, pork and poultry also are offered. Save room for the delectable desserts. The Sanderling has a full bar that includes a wide range of wines from around the world. A children's menu is available, and reservations are strongly encouraged. All three meals are served seven days a week throughout the year. The chef is always ready to accommodate any special dietary needs.

Cravings Coffee Shoppe
$ • Duck Common Shopping Center, N.C. Hwy. 12, Duck • (252) 261-0655

This delightful eatery is the perfect place to pop by for a quick breakfast before hitting the beach or to indulge yourself in a delectable dessert and coffee after dinner. You can eat inside, on an open-air deck or take the tasty treats home with you. Table service is not available; you order and pick up your food from the counter.

Order a fresh New York-style bagel with one of six flavored cream cheeses. Homemade pastries, breads and muffins also are baked each day. The ice cream is homemade as well. Out-of-town newspapers are also available each morning if you miss browsing through big city dailies such as *The Washington Post* and *The Wall Street Journal*.

For lunch, try an Italian sandwich on just-baked bread. Of course, every type of coffee drink you can concoct is available, from four types of brewed coffee that change daily to espresso, cappuccino, mocha drinks and other fancy combinations. You can also buy gourmet coffee beans, gift baskets and other items at a small shop inside Cravings. Cravings is open year round. In summer the eatery serves into the evening; it's open weekends only in winter.

The Village Wine Shop & Red Sky Cafe
$ • Village Square Shops, N.C. Hwy. 12, Duck • (252) 261-8646

This innovative cafe boasts the only wine bar on the beach and some of the best bread you'll enjoy anywhere. All bread and pizza are made on the premises in a wood-fired oven, and a wide variety of wines are available to sip by the glass. Along with the aromas emanating from the local organic herbs used in the food, the smell of the bread cooking is enough to get you salivating.

Owner/chef Tom Hix can whip up an impressively eclectic range in gourmet food: Mexican, French, Italian, Greek, Indian and Californian. The thin-crusted pizza with sun-dried tomatoes, pesto and fresh mozzarella cheese is out of this world. This is not ordinary pizza: This is heaven. It's the cafe's huge and unusually creative subs and sandwiches that pack the most punch, however. Our favorite is the Mt. Olympus, made with tomato, spinach, feta cheese, basil and marinated olives with pesto on French bread. Other inviting combos include Gavilanian Gobbler: smoked turkey, smoked Gouda, tomato, bacon, lettuce, red onion with Red Sky sauce on wheat bread; or Continental Divide: roast beef, bacon, monterey jack, coleslaw and red onion with barbecue sauce on sourdough bread. All sandwiches are reasonably priced and filling. Compared with vegetarian slim pickings at most eateries, the range of interesting vegetarian sandwiches — and meat lovers would swoon too — is wonderful.

For dinner, try a quesadilla or one of the four or five main courses that change nightly. Fresh Outer Banks seafood and pasta dishes are just two possibilities. Hix will be experimenting with a tapas-style menu in 1998, which will give diners a taste of the cafe's numerous specialties. An excellent selection of wine from all over the world can be purchased by the bottle or by the glass, and three microbrew beers are available on tap.

Interesting items can be found for sale on shelves lining this airy, very pleasant shop with wine racks, gourmet coffee and organic food products. The Village Wine Shop & Red Sky Cafe is open daily year round for lunch and dinner.

Elizabeth's Cafe & Winery
$$$ • Scarborough Faire, N.C. Hwy. 12, Duck • (252) 261-6145

Well known across the East Coast for its wine and wonderful food, Elizabeth's has earned international acclaim from *The Wine Spectator* magazine for consecutive years since 1991. For the past five years, this cafe was one of a handful in North Carolina to win Best of the Award of Excellence. In 1996 Elizabeth's was one of only 245 restaurants in the nation to win the honor. Owner Leonard Logan recently added a walk-in wine cellar and retail sales area and expanded the restaurant to accommodate handicapped patrons and to provide more room between tables.

Elizabeth's is a delight from ambiance to entrees. It's warm and casual inside, with a fireplace that's usually lit on chilly evenings. Service always is excellent, and the owner will personally select a vintage wine to complement any meal. Winemakers from around the world are featured here during special dinners held in August.

Besides the regular menu offerings, which include country French and California eclectic foods that change continually, prix-fixe dinners (seven-course meals and accompanying wines) are available every night in the summer. All the dishes are made with fresh ingredients, from seafood and steaks to unusual pastas. A new wine bar with cold appetizers, cheeses and croissants serves dining delights all afternoon and into the evening. A pastry chef also creates different desserts daily: Elizabeth's Craving is sinfully delicious.

This cafe is very popular, so reservations are highly recommended. On some summer weekends the owner has had to turn away as many as 500 potential diners. Besides all the fine wines, the restaurant also serves French beer by the glass, poured from wine-bottle-size containers. See our Nightlife chapter for more of Elizabeth's delights. The restaurant is open on weekends for dinner year round and for lunch and dinner seven days a week in-season.

Roadside Bar & Grill
$$ • N.C. Hwy. 12, Duck • (252) 261-5729

Occupying a renovated 1932 cottage, this 4-year-old restaurant is warm and homey, with hardwood floors inside and a patio dotted with umbrella-shaded tables out front. In the summer, live jazz and blues music is performed here three nights a week.

A casual, fine-dining establishment, Roadside offers 8-ounce burgers and crab cakes for lunch. The clam chowder is chock-full of shellfish, and a raw bar serving all sorts of shrimp, oysters and clam combinations is open all afternoon.

For dinner you can choose from fresh salads with mangos and other exotic fruits, loads of locally caught seafood, just sliced steaks, whole lobsters and poultry platters. Other specials change daily for lunch and dinner. Homemade desserts include chocolate bread pudding with Jack Daniels caramel sauce and steaming slices of Mom's Apple Pie. The full bar has a nice selection of microbrewed beers. The restaurant is open year round seven days a week. Reservations are not accepted.

The Blue Point Bar & Grill
$$$ • The Waterfront Shops, N.C. Hwy. 12, Duck • (252) 261-8090

This waterfront bistro is one of our favorite places to dine on the Outer Banks. It's been open for lunch and dinner since 1989 and consistently receives rave reviews from magazines such as *Southern Living* and *Gourmet* as well as admiring local audiences. Here, regional Southern cooking brings a cosmopolitan flair to the area. A 1950s-style interior with black-and-white checkered floors, red upholstery and lots of chrome provides an upbeat, bustling atmosphere. An enclosed porch not only overlooks the sound, it actually overhangs it. There's also a small bar facing the aromatic kitchen where you can watch your appetizers being prepared while sipping a cocktail as you wait for a table.

The Blue Point's menu is contemporary Southern cuisine and changes seasonally. Starters range from scallops to tuna cakes, each artistically arranged and flavored with the freshest combination of seasonings. Try the duck confit, slow-cooked meat on jalapeno corn bread with tamarind barbecue sauce. Entrees include jumbo lump crab cakes served with rice and black beans and Currituck corn on the cob, homemade soups, unusual seafood dishes, steaks, salads and perfect pastas. Desserts, like the bourbon pecan pie or the key lime pie, are divine.

If you're into creative cooking that's sure to tantalize every taste bud — and awaken some you might not even have realized you had — this restaurant is a must-stop on the Outer Banks. It's open for lunch and dinner year round, and reservations are highly recommended. In January, February and March, The Blue Point closes Mondays and Tuesdays. The eatery is also closed the first three weeks in December, but the rest of the year it's open seven days a week. Good thing — we're addicted!

Duck Deli
$ • N.C. Hwy. 12, Duck • (252) 261-3354

This casual deli on the east side of the highway opened 11 years ago primarily to serve locals lunch. Since then, it's expanded to offer breakfast, lunch and dinner seven days a week, 11 months of the year (the eatery closes during January).

Barbecue pork, beef, chicken and ribs are the specialities here. Sandwiches, Philly cheese steaks and subs are served all day, as are side salads, garden burgers and coleslaw. A full breakfast menu includes everything from eggs and pancakes to omelettes. For dessert, you can get sweet on cherry and peach cobblers, homemade brownies or a frozen yogurt bar with plenty of toppings. Beer is served at Duck Deli, and everything is available to eat in or take-out. Duck Deli is also the home of the booming Outer Banks business Carolina Blue Smoked Wildfish Co., whose gourmet food products are sold all over the country.

Swan Cove
$$$ • N.C. Hwy. 12, Duck • (252) 255-0500

This elegant establishment opened in 1995 and has gained a reputation as one of the finer establishments in Duck. Unbelievable views are available from the soundfront dining room, where tablecloths and cut flowers grace each table and crystal glasses sparkle during sunset hours. There's a separate lounge with a full bar and an extensive wine list upstairs.

The menu changes frequently to incorporate new offerings. Swan Cove uses all local produce, seafood and fresh herbs and specialize in low-fat, light cooking. Entrees include duck, pastas, French-cut pork chops, three kinds of Outer Banks fish, seafood bouillabaisse over saffron fettuccine, tenderloin steaks and fresh salads. Warm rolls and garden vegetables come with each dinner.

A great bet for starters: Shrimp stuffed with Gouda, wrapped in bacon and served with smoky barbecue sauce. For dessert, try choosing between a chocolate layer cake, peanut butter pie and seasonal fresh fruits drizzled with fabulous sauces.

Swan Cove is open seven days a week in-season, serving lunch and dinner; dinner only is served in spring and early fall. There is a children's menu. Reservations are suggested.

Southern Shores

Southern Bean

$, no credit cards • The Marketplace, U.S. Hwy. 158, MP 1, Southern Shores
• (252) 261 JAVA

Opened in September 1995, this gourmet coffee shop caters to folk looking for healthy light meals in addition to a great cup of brew. Southern Bean serves breakfast and lunch year round and adds dinner hours in the summer. Three types of just-brewed coffee always are simmering here, filling the air with tantalizing aromas.

This comfortable place serves every type of speciality coffee drink imaginable, from espresso and cappuccino to iced lattes — even in decaf varieties. More than 30 flavors of freshly roasted coffee beans are sold by the pound here. You can eat inside at Southern Bean, sip a warm blend at an outdoor table or order your drinks and food to go. All menu items are either vegetarian or seafood, and sandwiches range from hummus to peanut butter-and-honey; try the bean bagel topped with sun-dried tomatoes, pesto, red onion slices, cream cheese and sprouts. Muffins, croissants, cinnamon rolls and other bakery items also are available. No sandwich costs more than $5. This is also one of the few places on the Outer Banks where you can get fresh-squeezed juices and a wide variety of fruit smoothies.

Southern Bean is open seven days a week year round.

Kitty Hawk

Kitty Hawk Pier Restaurant
$, no credit cards • N.C. Hwy. 12, MP 1, Kitty Hawk • (252) 261-3151

One of the most popular breakfast places on the beach, this ultra-casual restaurant, which opened in 1954, is somewhere you'll feel comfortable just rolling out of bed and rolling into. Pancakes, eggs, sausage, French toast, omelettes, biscuits, hash browns, grits, sausage, bacon and anything else you could desire for a filling first meal of the day are cooked up beginning at 6 AM.

Lunch specials change daily and include such local favorites as ham and cabbage, trout, shrimp, crab cakes, meat loaf, and turkey with dressing and yams. For dinner, try a seafood platter of floun- der, scallops, oysters, dolphin or Spanish mackerel, each served with a choice of two sides: hush puppies, rolls, coleslaw, beets, peas, beans or other vegetables.

Kitty Hawk Pier Restaurant is a down-home place with lots of local patrons and flavor. You can find out what's biting here and even may see your dinner being reeled in off the nearby wooden planks. Most of the fish are caught right off the pier, within 200 feet of where you eat it. Better still, you can come as you are — even in your bathing suit.

Desserts include homemade cobblers (peach, apple, blueberry and cherry), strawberry shortcake and a variety of pies. A children's menu is offered for the small fry. Everything is available to take out, but you'll enjoy eating in this oceanfront restaurant where salt spray stains the wide windows.

The restaurant serves three meals a day every day in summer. In the off-season only breakfast and lunch are available. Kitty Hawk Pier Restaurant is open April through November.

Rundown Cafe
$$ • N.C. Hwy. 12, MP 1, Kitty Hawk • (252) 255-0026

Opened in 1993, this Caribbean-style cafe has been a big hit with locals who live on the northern end of the beach and offers some spicy, unusual alternatives to traditional Outer Banks seafood. Named for a Jamaican stew, Rundown serves island entrees flavored with African and Indian accents. Try the conch chowder for an appetizer or one of several wild soups that change seasonally.

Specials shift nightly. Some of our favorites are blackened pork tenderloin, spinach-and-feta-stuffed chicken with roasted red pepper sauce and freshly grilled tuna topped with sesame vinaigrette. The steam bar here serves shellfish of all sorts, vegetables and steamed dinners. All the regular menu items also are terrific.

There's a full bar, and the bartenders can come up with some pretty potent concoctions. And there's Guinness Stout, Bass and Harp beers on tap. This is a casual, happening place often features live blues and jazz in the summer (see our Nightlife chapter). A rooftop deck is a great place to soak in the sunset, catch a few rays or just linger over a cool cocktail after a hot day in the sun. Lunch and dinner are available seven days a week. The Rundown is closed in December.

Ocean Boulevard
$$$ • N.C. Hwy. 12, MP 2, Kitty Hawk • (252) 261-2546

This warm, cozy, upscale eatery gives you a great feeling from the second you walk into the gold-walled dining room until you leave full and relaxed after consuming a fabulous meal. It opened in September 1995 and has quickly become one of the most popular places on the Outer Banks. Manteo residents drive 30 miles each way to treat themselves to a midweek dinner here. No wonder — it's owned by the same culinary masters who brought us the Blue Point in Duck (see previous entry). Ocean Boulevard has an intimate atmosphere, and the food is sophisticated.

This restaurant occupies the former 1949 Virginia Dare Hardware store, and you won't believe what the builders and decorators have done with the place. It's accented with warm woods, burgundy fabrics and forest-green chairs. Cobalt blue glasses and water pitchers grace every table top. There's even an open-air kitchen where you can watch the chefs work.

Selections are all prepared with locally grown herbs, spices, produce and just-caught seafood. Influences and ideas from around the world give the food here a flavor all its own, and the menu changes according to the season. For an appetizer, try seared rare tuna served with wasabi coleslaw and soy honey glaze. Four meal-size salads, one with seven types of lettuce, also are outstanding.

Entrees like cornmeal-crusted sea bass with roasted vegetables and black olive tapanade or macadamia-crusted mahi mahi served with rum-baked beans with passion fruit butter sauce are exquisite. And you can't go wrong by ordering any of the pastas, beef, shrimp with Portobello mushrooms or pork chops served with blue cornmeal onion rings.

Ocean Boulevard's wine list contains more than 100 selections, at least a dozen of which are served by the glass. Microbrewed beers and a full bar also are on hand. Six dessert offerings each are to die for. We especially crave the white chocolate crème brûlée, The Blvd., and macadamia nut torte with caramel ice cream. A full line of after-dinner coffee drinks and herbal teas also is served.

This elegant eatery will please even the most discriminating diners. It's open year round for dinner only. During summers, doors are open seven days a week. Call for off-season hours. Reservations are highly recommended.

Keeper's Galley
$$ • U.S. Hwy. 158, MP 4, Kitty Hawk • (252) 261-4000

Keeper's Galley now is run by Rufus Pritchard Jr., the same fellow who owns the Dunes Restaurant in Nags Head (see subsequent entry). But the menu is slightly different here, and Keeper's Galley serves breakfast, lunch and dinner seven days a week in-season.

Breakfast, which is available until noon, features waffles, eggs, pancakes, country ham, grits, toast, biscuits, vegetarian breakfast sandwiches and fish roe stirred into eggs. For lunch, try a Reuben, cold plate, shrimp or tuna sandwich, homemade seafood gumbo or a big bowl of clam chowder. Dinner entrees change daily but include such regular offerings as prime rib, crab cakes, seafood fettuccine, chicken and a surf and turf platter. For dessert, the turtle cake is simply scrumptious. Keeper's Galley has a children's menu and a full bar. Reservations aren't accepted.

John's Drive-In
$, no credit cards • N.C. Hwy. 12, MP 4¾, Kitty Hawk • (252) 261-2916

Home of the planet's best milk shakes, John's has been an Outer Banks institution for years. Some folk even drive two hours from Norfolk just to sip one of the thick fruit and ice cream concoctions, some of which won't even flow through the straw. Our favorite is the chocolate-peanut butter-and-banana variety, but you'll have to sample a few first and create some of your own combinations before making that call for yourself.

You can't eat inside here, but plenty of picnic tables across from the ocean are scattered around the old concrete building. Everything is served in paper bags to go. While you're waiting for your food, check out the faded photographs of happy customers who line the salt-sprayed windows of this diner. You may even recognize a few local friends.

Besides the milk shakes and ice cream sundae treats, John's serves delicious dolphin, trout and tuna sandwiches or boats with the fish crispy-fried alongside crinkle fries. Dogs love this drive-in too. If your pooch waits patiently in the car, the worker behind the window probably will provide him or her with a free "puppy" cup of soft-serve vanilla ice cream. We can't think of a better doggie treat on a hot summer afternoon.

John's drive-in is open from May through October for lunch and early dinner. It's closed Wednesdays, unfortunately (we could eat there seven days a week).

Tradewinds
$ • U.S. Hwy. 158, MP 4½, Kitty Hawk • (252) 261-3052

If you're in the mood for Chinese food, Tradewinds serves tasty Mandarin-style dishes. The chef here is willing to cook each meal to your specification, whether you prefer lightly steamed vegetables without a sauce or a variation on the seafood, chicken and beef entrees, which are always available. Carry-out is popular here, as it is at many Chinese restaurants, but the generous portions of succulent spicy and mild meals are best enjoyed in this dimly lighted eatery. Tradewinds has a full bar and is open for lunch and dinner all year.

Kill Devil Hills

JK's Ribs
$ • U.S. Hwy. 158, MP 5¼, Kill Devil Hills • (252) 441-9555

Long known for serving the best pork ribs on the beach, JK's originally opened in the early 1980s, but the restaurant burned down several years later. Now, JK and his gang are back in a tiny eatery at the Grass Course. Again, they're serving those baby back ribs that have made mouths water for years. There's no table service here; you have to call in carry-out orders or pick up your own plate from the counter. A few tables allow you to eat inside, and outdoor tables are available too. Besides ribs, which are smothered in his famous dry spice so you don't have to deal with sloppy sauce, JK's serves grilled and roasted chicken, hamburgers, cold salads, coleslaw, red beans, freshly baked corn bread and thick brownies. Beer and wine are available. You can eat lunch and dinner here year round, including late night suppers. Limited delivery also is available with a minimum $12 order. Reservations are not accepted.

Chilli Peppers
$$ • U.S. Hwy. 158, MP 5½, Kill Devil Hills • (252) 441-8081

World fusion with a Southwestern twist comes alive in the cooking at this fun, always bustling restaurant. Owner Jim Douglas has worked in Outer Banks eateries for years and has brought some of the most creative cooking around to Chilli Peppers. If being adventuresome is your style, you'll be wowed by the chefs' wild collaborations. If you prefer a milder meal, they can do that too and still tickle some untapped taste buds. The menu here changes frequently, with daily lunch and dinner specials sometimes stunning even the regulars. Some of our favorite entrees are the scallops, steak, shrimp, pork and quail combinations, each as tastefully presented as they are tasty. Chefs Damon Krasauskas and Kenny McClean, both graduates of renowned culinary schools, always come up with something exciting. The nachos appetizer is a meal in itself.

A full bar separate from the cozy dining room offers fresh-fruit Margaritas, a nice wine selection and more than a dozen varieties of bottled beer. Nonalcoholic fruit smoothies also are a great bet in the early afternoon. Steamed seafood and veggies are served until closing. There's usually something going on here late night (see our Nightlife chapter) too. Chilli Peppers is an extremely progressive restaurant with a laid-back feel. Cacti, wooden chairs and hand-painted accents all add to the casual atmosphere. Lunch and dinner are served here seven days a week year round. Weekend brunches, featuring a make-your-own Bloody Mary bar, are worth getting out of bed for. Also, you can take home a bottle of Chilli's award-winning original hot sauce, barbecue sauce or hot salt. The T-shirts, too, make great memorabilia of a delicious meal.

Awful Arthur's

$$ • N.C. Hwy. 12, MP 6, Kill Devil Hills • (252) 441-5955

An always-popular spot across from Avalon Pier, this raw bar and restaurant is usually crowded throughout the year. Wooden tables are laid out along the oblong room, and a bar stretches the entire length of the downstairs eatery. Upstairs, a separate lounge offers an ocean view. A live lobster tank and huge saltwater reef tank also offer interesting sea creatures to watch as you dine.

Arthur's is a comfortably casual place where you won't mind peeling seasoned shrimp or picking the meat from succulent crab legs with sticky fingers. Seafood is the speciality here: Everything from scallops and oysters to clams, mussels, homemade crab cakes and daily entree specials. The bartenders are some of the fastest shuckers in town. Bass Ale and several other varieties of beer are on tap, or you can order from a full line of liquor and speciality drinks. For landlubbers, several non-seafood sandwiches are served.

At night, Arthur's is usually packed. A late night menu is available. Mondays are Locals' Nights, featuring drink and food specials all day. Arthur's T-shirts have been seen all over the world and are also local favorites. This eatery is open seven days a week year round for lunch and dinner.

La Fogata Mexican Restaurant

$ • U.S. Hwy. 158, MP 4½, Kitty Hawk • (252) 255-0934
$ • U.S. Hwy. 158, MP 14½, Nags Head • (252) 441-4179

A traditional Mexican restaurant, La Fogata got its name from the Spanish word for "campfire." All the owners, waiters and cooks are Mexican natives, but almost all of them speak English. We think they serve the best ethnic food for the price on the beach. After being open for four years, people still wait in line to eat here on weekend nights.

Airy, bright and decorated with paper piñatas, the interior of this ultra-casual eatery usually hums with Latin tunes; a mariachi band plays here frequently. Tables and booths all are set with bowls of slightly spicy homemade salsa, and the waiters never stop filling the baskets of crispy tortillas they serve as soon as they distribute the menus. Beware: We often fill up on chips and this authentic salsa before the meals arrive. All entree portions are generous, so save some room for the main course. Other appetizers we enjoy include the hot queso (cheese) dip and stuffed jalapeno peppers.

Specialties here are fajitas, beef and chicken tacos, enchiladas and chiles rellenos. The cooks make the dishes hot or mild, depending on your desire. Selections come in every possible combination, vegetarian varieties and à la carte if you want to try one of everything. (Actually, that's impossible here. The menu has more than 36 dinner selections, many starting at $6.) A full bar offers a wide selection of Mexican, American and imported beers, and mixed-drink and Margarita prices are among the lowest on the beach. La Fogata is open for lunch and dinner year round, seven days a week.

3rd Street Oceanfront Grille
$$$ • Sea Ranch Hotel, N.C. Hwy. 12, MP 7, Kill Devil Hills • (252) 441-7126

3rd Street Oceanfront Grille offers one of the few true oceanfront dining rooms on the Outer Banks. A wall of glass overlooks the Atlantic, allowing patrons at any table to get caught up in the rhythm of the waves. The menu features traditional Outer Banks seafood and steaks prepared with a Southern regional flair. Appetizers include fried green tomatoes with a remoulade sauce; grilled shrimp and grits with sauteed sweet peppers and red-eye gravy; and puff pastries filled with sauteed scallops, country ham, mushrooms and spinach in a Chardonnay shallot cream sauce.

A children's menu and nightly specials are available. Our favorite entrees include fresh egg fettuccine with scallops and shrimp tossed with bacon, sweet peas and a garlic cream sauce; grilled center-cut pork chop with an apple pecan compote; and sesame seed-crusted wahoo with a wilted spinach and soy ginger beurre blanc. The selections and service here are superb. A traditional breakfast also is served daily, and Sunday Brunch is served until noon every week. 3rd Street isn't open for lunch, and reservations are recommended for dinner. The restaurant is open seven days a week year round.

Great Dane Deli & Wrong Dog Cafe
$$ • Dare Centre, U.S. Hwy. 158, MP 7, Kill Devil Hills • (252) 441-2519

Formerly Petrozza's deli, this new eatery/delicatessen serves New York-style salads, sandwiches and bakery goods that will make Northeastern visitors feel at home and local Southerners appreciate what they've missed. With one of the largest deli sandwich selections on the beach, this cafe provides every kind of combination a hungry patron would want.

The menu carries the cafe's colorful canine name to its fun and creative heights. Every item is named for some kind of dog and is elaborated with a humorous play on words. It's a clever gimmick, because you can't resist reading through the whole menu. Once you do, you won't be able to decide which mouthwatering combo to order. How about the Bloodhound ("this sandwich can't miss, it'll track YOU down"), Black Forest ham and melted dill havarti cheese with mayo, Dijon mustard and onion on rye bread? Or the Greyhound ("big and fast and lean . . . bet on this one!"), lean pork sausage and seared bell peppers and onions with marinara sauce and melted mozzarella cheese on a half-loaf of Italian bread, served hot. There's even the Wright Dog (two beef franks on a poppy seed roll) and the Wrong Dog (a vegetarian sandwich with pesto sauce).

You can eat in or take-out at the Wrong Dog Cafe, but if you're looking for a nice break in the day, we suggest having a seat. The black-and-white checkerboard linoleum and unobtrusive, tasteful decor make this cafe a comfortable spot to relish a satisfying meal alone or with a friend. There's plenty worth taking home, also, including a range of gourmet pasta and vegetable salads, fantastic crusty breads and delectable desserts. A good selection of fine wine is also available to purchase. Dinner entrees, which include fresh bread, an appetizer sampler and a family-style salad, range from fettuccine Alfredo to chicken marsala to shrimp Florentine. Entrees can be ordered for take-out, also. Espresso, cappuccino, beer and wine are some of the drink options.

The Great Dane Deli & Wrong Dog Cafe is open Tuesday through Thursday from 11 AM to 7 PM. On Friday and Saturday the eatery is open until 8 PM.

Goombay's Grille & Raw Bar
$$ • N.C. Hwy. 12, MP 7½, Kill Devil Hills • (252) 441-6001

A fun place for food, drinks and just hanging out, Goombay's is owned by John Kirchmier, a 16-year veteran of Outer Banks restaurants and bars. "Good days and nights can always be found at Goombay's" is the fitting motto of this island-style eatery. Light and bright inside, with plenty of cool artwork, there's an outrageous fish tank and a wall-size tropical mural in the dining room. The ambiance is upbeat and casual, with wooden tables and chairs and a bare tile floor. The horseshoe-shaped bar, which is separate from the eating area, is a great place to try some of the delicious appetizers or drink specials that Goombay's serves. We especially recommend the spicy crab balls and sweet coconut shrimp. Some of the drink offerings, both alcoholic and children's cocktails, come with zany toys to take home.

For lunch or dinner, try a fresh pasta entree, locally caught seafood, a juicy burger topped as you wish, Southwestern sampling or one of the half-dozen daily specials that range from pork to barbecued shrimp and steak stir-fry. Everything here is reasonably priced and flavorful. A raw bar is open until 1 AM, serving steamed shrimp, oysters, vegetables and other favorites. Key lime pie is always a smart choice for dessert. Goombay's is open for lunch and dinner year round, seven days a week (see our Nightlife chapter).

Quagmires
$$ • N.C. Hwy. 12, MP 7½, Kill Devil Hills • (252) 441-9188

With two oceanfront decks, an upstairs snack bar and large downstairs dining room overlooking the Atlantic, Quagmires is entering its third summer season. It's owned and operated by John Kirchmier, who's already locally revered for his Goombay's Grille (see previous entry).

This casual restaurant caters to almost every dining whim. If you're sunning yourself on the beach midday and start to hear your stomach grumble, you can get lunch to go from the upstairs grill without even putting on shoes or throwing a shirt over your wet bathing suit. If you'd rather wait to dress for dinner, you'll feel well cared for — and fed — in the casual downstairs dining room. The giant U-shaped bar upstairs provides a great place to watch the waves and sip some of the best Margaritas and frozen drinks on the beach. There's a kid's menu and special treats just for the little ones. A volleyball court, horseshoe pit and even ring toss are set up in the sand behind this eatery in case the younger set gets bored while their folks dawdle over dinner. Don't be misled, though: Those games also are open to adults. Better still, in 1998 Quagmire's has added a new kids' playground.

The menu here features fresh local seafood, sandwiches, pasta, beef, chicken and some Mexican favorites. The desserts are fresh and fabulous. Live acoustic music is offered throughout the summer (see our Nightlife chapter). Quagmires is open seven days a week for lunch and dinner in-season.

The Thai Room
$$ • Oceanside Plaza, N.C. Hwy. 12, MP 8½, Kill Devil Hills • (252) 441-1180

Jimmy lets his patrons choose their own level of spice — from mild to blow-your-brains-out. When he asks, "Very hot?" — think twice. He means it. Besides the daily specials, the cooks have added a new buffet dinner so you can sample several of the wonderful offerings. More than a dozen American-style desserts are available. As for decor, it is unlike any other on North Carolina's barrier islands: authentically Thai with paper lanterns, Oriental portraits and red-tasseled lamps. Family members prepare and serve each delectable meal — and they'll be happy to make suggestions if you're overwhelmed by all the options. The Thai Room is open for lunch and dinner March through December. All items also are available for carry-out. The restaurant also has a full bar where you can indulge in exotic drinks and Thai beer while you wait for a table or take-out order.

Bob's Grill
$ • U.S. Hwy. 158, MP 9, Kill Devil Hills • (252)441-0707

Bob's is open year round for breakfast, lunch and dinner. During the summer it also stays open from dinner straight through breakfast the next day from Wednesday through Saturday. Bob serves big, cheap breakfasts year round seven days a week until 3 PM daily — and that's hard to find around here. The blueberry pancakes are so big, they fill a whole plate. Eggs are made any way you want 'em, and the hash browns flavored with onions and peppers are some of the best around.

For lunch, try a hamburger, tuna steak or one of several traditional hot and cold sandwiches. Owner Bob McCoy cooks much of the food himself. A hot lunch special for $4.92, tax and drink included, is available every day. You can't leave town without trying Bob's No. 1 seller — Philly steak and cheese. Dinners feature the biggest cuts of prime rib on the Outer Banks, Cajun beer batter-dipped shrimp and fresh mahi mahi caught just offshore. The selection of salads is also good here. And you gotta save room for the hot fudge brownie dessert.

Bob's has a casual, diner-like atmosphere, with a regular-folk appeal that makes everyone comfortable. Even McCoy's well-known gruff motto, "Eat and get the hell out," has obviously not offended any locals, since the parking lot is packed with loyal customers more days than not. Service is fast and friendly, beer and wine are available, and everything can be ordered for carry-out. This grill closes from 3 to 5 PM daily, but it's open for three meals a day every day all year and overnight on summer weekends.

Chardo's

$$ • U.S. Hwy. 158, MP 9, Kill Devil Hills • (252) 441-0276

Owner Ron Chinappi is continuing the tradition of fine dining begun a decade ago by his father Rich Chinappi, a first-generation Italian American. Chardo's provides a cultural as well as culinary experience at this family-run establishment.

A quiet, fine restaurant specializing in seafood and meats with regional flavors of Italy, Chardo's serves an array of entrees and plenty of homemade pasta. Whether you're in the mood for spaghetti and meatballs or traditional Italian seafood, Chardo's will satisfy your palate. Veal chops are a speciality here, cut to order on the premises. There's a $9.95 steak and pasta special each Tuesday, Thursday and Sunday. Fresh sauteed or steamed vegetables and warm bread accompanies every entree.

Salads here are prepared with originality and flair. They include an interesting combination of garden vegetables and flavorful homemade dressings. The tableside Caesar salad especially is delicious. A full bar is set apart from the dining area. Chardo's wine list features top California and Italian varieties, and a coffee bar also is on hand for after-dinner speciality drinks. All the desserts are made daily; try a cannoli, tiramisu or napoleon for the perfect ending to a delightful dinner. Children can purchase half-portions of any entree for half-price. Several smaller rooms set off from the main dining area provide an intimate atmosphere for special occasions.

Chardo's sells specialty Italian meats, cheeses, breads and imported olive oil you can take home, and the restaurant caters. Chardo's is open all year for dinner. Call for winter hours.

Dare Devil's Authentic Pizzeria

$ • N.C. Hwy. 12, MP 9, Kill Devil Hills • (252) 441-6330, (252) 441-2353

This pizza parlor has been in business for more than a decade and is known for its superb strombolis and hand-tossed pizzas. Chicken wings, mozzarella sticks, nachos, Greek salads and pizza bread also are available here. Dare Devil's also has four types of beer on tap served in frosty glass mugs. The interior is low-key, with laminated tables and a long bar where you can eat. A big-screen TV in the corner features whatever hot sporting event happens to be going on. You can also order any item to take out. Dare Devil's is open seven days a week for lunch and dinner from March through November.

Pigman's Bar-B-Que
$ • U.S. Hwy. 158, MP 9½, Kill Devil Hills • (252) 441-6803

Pigman's rib-man, Bill Shaver, is locally famous for his corny cable television commercials. He's also known for serving succulent North Carolina-style barbecue and walking his pet potbellied pigs around town. At this counter-service eatery, you can get beef, pork, chicken, and ribs barbecue. Try his new low-fat creations: catfish, turkey and tuna barbecue. Each dinner comes with homemade coleslaw, homemade hush puppies and baked beans and is served on disposable plates with plastic utensils. The sweet potato fries here are spectacular. Pigman's has a selection of gorgeous Southwestern jewelry and gifts for sale. You can also purchase his hush puppy mix, all four Pigman barbecue sauces and Pigman meat rub at the restaurant. Pigman's is open for lunch and dinner seven days a week. It's closed January and February. Come on by and visit Pigman's critters behind the building. You might see one of his llamas, his miniature donkey or horse, or one of his smart, lovable potbellied pigs.

Peppercorns
$$ • Ramada Inn, N.C. Hwy. 12, MP 9, Kill Devil Hills • (252) 441-2151

With a wide, open dining room overlooking the Atlantic, Peppercorns and its team of chefs supervised by Ramada Inn Food and Beverage Director Robin Rector has been attracting the most discerning diners on the Outer Banks. Up-and-coming culinary master Randy Stitt is the sous chef. Mark Pennington offers multi-ethnic foods and aromatic Mediterranean dishes as the chef de cuisine. And executive chef Erik Speer brings a cosmopolitan flair to the entire menu with innovative appetizers, healthy grilled entrees and an array of finely crafted desserts.

Outer Banks favorites include locally caught shrimp and crab cakes. The soup du jour is always filling and delicious. Unusual dishes flavored with saffron, curry, Thai spices and chiles also will tempt those with extraordinary tastes. Entrees include prime rib crusted with spices, slow-roasted and served au jus; Atlantic salmon stuffed with crabmeat; or Italian risotto with shrimp, scallops and crabmeat. Each meal is served with several artfully prepared vegetables and a basket of interesting breads. Vegetarian entrees always are offered. There's a full bar and a children's menu. You'll especially want to save room for Erik's painted-plate desserts, some of which are so carefully manicured they appear as masterpieces after the artistically arranged meals. The seven-layer chocolate cake,

New York-style cheesecake with a raspberry coulis or apple dumplings served with cinnamon caramel sauce will leave your palate begging for more. Peppercorns provides take-out food and room service for Ramada guests. This restaurant is open daily year round for breakfast, lunch and dinner. Custom catering also is available for events of any size.

Flying Fish Cafe
$$ • U.S. Hwy. 158, MP 10, Kill Devil Hills • (252) 441-6894
This delightful restaurant is owned by George Price, who helped manage Penguin Isle for eight years before he decided to open his own restaurant. John Xenakis and Price purchased the former Osprey Island Grille, sandblasted off its pink and teal exterior and added their own special touches, and dishes, to create an island eatery serving an array of American and Mediterranean dishes. The interior is spruce green and adobe white with purple accents. Price's color photographs grace the walls. Brightly colored tablecloths adorn each table, illuminated by sconce wall lights crafted from wine boxes and by candles set in the center of each table or booth.

Chefs at Flying Fish roll their own pasta daily and offer an array of seafood, vegetarian and nontraditional toppings for the scrumptious noodles. Gourmet pot pies, salmon and roasted chicken are also always on the menu. Fresh fish is served four ways each night, and there's an Angus filet mignon and pork chops with caramelized onions for meat lovers. All entrees come with a starch of the day, vegetables and just-baked bread. Appetizers include Portobello mushrooms stuffed with shrimp, two types of soup, oysters Florentine and hot seafood dip. For dessert, try to resist the Grecian Urn, a waffle filled with ice cream and topped with glazed fresh fruit and whipped cream. Chocoholics will love the chocolate hurricane, a bed of chocolate with dark chocolate swirled through the top.

Lunch specials are served daily. And more than 40 types of wine are served by the bottle or glass. A children's menu also is available. Early bird dinner specials are discounted from 5 to 6 PM. The Flying Fish offers lunch and dinner every day year round. Reservations are recommended for dinner at this casual, innovative restaurant.

Millie's Diner
$$ • N.C. Hwy. 12, MP 10, Kill Devil Hills • (252) 480-3463
A fully restored 1940s dining car, Millie's made a hit from the moment it was delivered to the beach in summer 1996. Gleaming

silver, Millie's initially attracted attention for its classy retro look. But it quickly got more notice for its gourmet menu. Food at Millie's is creative, distinctive and delicious. And considering the upbeat decor inside — art deco set off by burgundy and yellow walls and room fixings — this is a most extraordinary and satisfying place to dine.

Note the authentic 1950s jukeboxes (stocked with jazz, blues, funk and rock) in each of the dining room's eight booths. The dinner menu offers both light fare — which includes pan seared scallops with Portobello mushrooms, plum tomatoes and carmelized shallots; or Millie's bruschetti with roma tomatoes, smoked mozzarella, sweet basil and olive oil — and full-blown entrees such as grilled Moroccan spiced New York strip with wild mushrooms and creamy potato gratin or Parmesan-crusted tuna with sage, basil and lemon butter. Other offerings, which change according to availability and season, include vegetable and polenta torte with eggplant, summer squash, tomatoes and roasted red pepper sauce and nightly fresh seafood specials.

The homemade desserts are no less imaginative. Selections have included such delights as steamed ginger pudding with butterscotch sauce. Lunch menu items include grilled Asian-spiced salmon with sesame noodles and spicy beef and mushroom burrito, in addition to out-of-the-ordinary sandwiches. Breakfast is added to the menu after Easter. And Millie's "World Famous" brunch, offered Saturday and Sunday in the off-season and every day in the summer, is all you could ever want in a brunch — fabulous omelettes, thick French toast with berries and cream, steak and eggs, mouthwatering salads, grilled quesadillas and wonderful specials.

Millie's prides itself in using the freshest food available, including organic produce, so the menu is flexible. An extensive wine list, imported, domestic and microbrewed beers and a full bar are available. Millie's also offers live music in the summer (see our Nightlife chapter). Millie's is open April through November. The diner serves daily in the summer, and six days a week in the off-season.

Colington Island

Colington Cafe
$$ • Colington Rd., 1 mile west of U.S. Hwy. 158, Kill Devil Hills • (252) 480-1123
   Step back in time at this cozy Victorian cafe, nestled among live

oaks on Colington Road. This popular restaurant is only a mile off the Bypass. Once you've arrived, you'll feel worlds away from the bustling beach. It's tranquil and absolutely lovely in this restored old home set high on a hill. This is our favorite place to come for an intimate dinner, and the chefs prepare some of the most marvelous meals around for extremely reasonable prices. Three small dining rooms are adorned in tasteful decor. There's a separate bar upstairs where you can sip a glass of wine or imported beer while waiting for your table. Even the black painted plates are unusual and artistic.

Hot crab dip slathered on buttery crackers and bowls of home-made crab bisque are outstanding appetizers. Daily specials include wonderful pasta dishes, a mixed grill with hollandaise and the fresh-est filet mignon available. Seafood entrees change depending on what's just been caught. Only fresh herbs and vegetables are used in cooking and as side dishes. Salads are served à la carte.

Owner Carlen Pearl's French heritage permeates her restaurant's delicious cream sauces, and she makes most of the irresistible des-serts herself — from blackberry cobbler to chocolate tortes and crème brûlée. Colington Cafe is open for dinner only seven days a week, April through November. In the off-season, the cafe is open Christmas week and Thursday through Sunday from Valentine's Day through April 1.

Bridges Neighborhood Bar & Bistro
$$ • 1469 Colington Rd., Colington • (252) 441-6398

Drive west three minutes from the bustling Bypass on winding two-lane Colington Road, and you'll be in the thick of Colington's charm. Bridges, a frame house tucked among tangled bushes and small gardens adjacent to a skinny canal, is just right for those who want to relax in an unpretentious, friendly atmosphere. Good food at affordable prices can be had at this homey bistro. Diners can relax with a drink before or after dinner on a screened-in porch that overlooks the canal. Inside, booths afford comfort while en-joying a meal in the light and airy dining room. Appetizers include seafood fritters with Cajun mayonnaise and mushroom ravioli with peanut ginger sauce. Lunch ranges from meat loaf with mashed potatoes, shrimp jambalaya or pasta of the day. Sandwiches like pork barbecue, sliced steak with grilled onion, fried oyster, fried fish and marinated grilled portobello mushroom are available day or night, and are served with a choice of fries, potato salad or baked beans. Seafood dinners, served with fries, coleslaw and hush puppies, are available after 5 PM. Seasonal entrees are other options: roasted pork loin chops with corn-bread stuffing, apple gravy and vegetables; half-chicken, roasted with garlic and rosemary, potato and a vegetable; or linguine with shrimp, feta and Bridges' marinara. Homemade dessert, soup and salad are also on the menu, as well as a good selection of bottled wine, wine-by-the-glass and domestic, imported and microbrewed beers. Bridges is open from 11:30 AM to 10 PM every day year round.

Nags Head

Red Drum Taphouse
$$ • N.C. Hwy. 12, MP 10, Nags Head • (252) 480-1095

New in 1998, the Red Drum earned word-of-mouth praise from the moment it opened. The handsome red brick exterior presents an apt introduction to the very tasteful decor inside: glossy, deep rust-colored square tables, a gleaming redwood bar stretching across the back wall, big windows, a poster-size photo of an angler with his red drum catch, even a small fireplace that makes things cozy on cooler days.

Red Drum also serves up tasteful food. For lunch try chowder, wings or shrimp con queso for starters. Follow with more filling fare, including steamed snow crab legs, burgers, crab-cake sandwich, chicken havarti, fish and chips or a blue-plate special that changes daily.

Dinner offerings include cowboy steak, a 16-ounce bone-in Angus rib steak, grilled and served with Red Drum onion rings; apple chops, a double pork porterhouse chop grilled with a hard cider glaze, served with sweet potato gratin and veggies; or bangers and mash, grilled banger served over sour cream mashed potatoes with a Portobello mushroom gravy and veggies.

Grilled or fried fresh fish, pasta and vegetarian dishes are also available on this unique menu.

Sunday brunch is also served in-season after Easter. In addition to traditional items like omelettes and French toast, Red Drum also serves up mom-style chicken and dumplings, meat loaf, and poached egg over prime rib.

Red Drum serves lunch and dinner year round. Closing times — 10 PM weekdays and 10:30 PM weekends — are extended into the wee hours with entertainment. (See our Nightlife chapter.)

Kelly's Outer Banks Restaurant & Tavern

$$$ • U.S. Hwy. 158, MP 10½, Nags Head • (252) 441-4116

Kelly's is an Outer Banks tradition and one of the most popular restaurants year round. Owner Mike Kelly gives his personal attention to every detail, so the service and selections are always first-rate. This is a large, upscale eatery and a busy place. The decor reflects the area's rich maritime heritage and includes abundant examples of fish, birds and other wildlife. The tavern is hopping seven nights a week, even during winter (see our Nightlife chapter).

Dinner is the only meal served here, and it's offered in several rooms upstairs and downstairs. Kelly's menu offers fresh seafood dishes, chicken, beef and pastas. There's a raw bar for those who enjoy feasting on oysters and other steamed shellfish. An assortment of delicious homemade breads accompanies each meal. Kelly's sweet potato biscuits are succulent — we usually ask for a second basket. Desserts are flavorful and filling. A separate children's menu is available, complete with crayons and special placemats to color. Kelly's also caters private parties, weddings and any style event imaginable. The restaurant and lounge are open daily. Dinner is served between 5 PM and 10 PM.

New York Pizza Pub

$ • U.S. Hwy. 158 MP 10, Nags Head • (252) 441-2660

Spacious and welcoming, New York Pizza Pub offers — you guessed it — all the Italian food favorites you'd find in the Northeast. Its motto, "the ultimate family feast," is reflected in a menu that offers a wide range of selections: steaks, fresh seafood, pasta dishes, calzones, salads and soups. And of course, there's pizza — traditional hand-tossed, Chicago deep-dish, Sicilian or pan pizza is available in 19 gourmet styles. Try one laden with fresh broccoli, spinach, oven-roasted peppers, mushrooms, onions, garlic, ricotta, marinara and a pound of mozzarella cheese.

Sandwiches, heros, burgers and stuffed potatoes are also available. Specialty coffees and desserts can top it all off — if you have any room left. Or you can choose a domestic, imported or microbrewed beer or a glass or bottle of imported or domestic wine.

New York Pizza Pub is open year round for lunch and dinner.

Mrs. T's Deli

$ • U.S. Hwy. 158, MP 10, Nags Head • (252) 441-1220

Owned and operated by a little local lady, her sweet daughter Shirley and two grandchildren when school lets out, this homey deli is a great bet for quick, satisfying lunches and some of the friendliest chatter in town. A big color TV plays year-old movies constantly, and the largest collection of antique cookie jars we've ever seen lines three walls. You serve yourself drinks here out of a wall of coolers stocked with everything from beer and Snapple to sodas and exotic fruit drinks. Menu items are scrawled in thick magic marker strokes on paper plates and cardboard squares hung behind the cash register.

Mrs. T's soups are laden with vegetables, pulled chicken and rich broth. Most of her three-dozen sandwiches are named after friends and family members who eat here. We like the Stacy sub with four types of melted cheese. And the three varieties of veggie burgers always get rave reviews. Club sandwiches are stacked so high they barely fit in your mouth. And all the meats and cheeses are fresh out of the deli counter, which also offers items by the half-pound or more to take home. The Outer Banks curly fries, lightly seasoned and made to order, are wonderful. Each entree comes with ripple chips and a pickle. Cakes, pastries and gourmet jelly beans are available for dessert, and lots of kosher food, including matzos, can be found all year. Mrs. T's serves lunch and dinner seven days a week from mid-March through early February. Everything here can be packaged to go.

Tortuga's Lie Shellfish Bar & Grille

$ • N.C. Hwy. 12, MP 11, Nags Head • (252) 441-RAWW

Our hands-down favorite haunt on the Outer Banks, this small, upbeat eatery is housed in a turquoise and white cottage across from the ocean near a great surf break. Tortuga's features an enclosed porch furnished with handmade wooden booths; an expanded bar seats more than two-dozen people. There's a sand volleyball court out back where pickup games always are being played — and watched from the outdoor picnic tables. This is one of the only places around where it's truly comfortable to eat alone. The bartenders and wait staff are some of the friendliest folk we know. The food is fabulous and creatively concocted. The atmosphere inside is fun and casual, with turtle-themed batiks hanging from the white walls and more than 100 license plates, some with pretty unusual personal messages, from across the country tacked to the low ceiling beams.

The menu here offers everything from 'gator bites — yes, the real thing — and delicious sandwiches to scrumptious seafood flavored with outrageous spices and a full raw bar that always has something steaming. The french fries are the best we've ever had. And the coco loco chicken entree (smothered with coconut, served with a side of lime curry dipping sauce for lunch and dinner) is something we crave at least once a week. Other dinner entrees include pork medallions, steak stir-fries, just-off-the-boat tuna steaks, succulent shrimp and pasta plates. Most meals come with finely flavored rice and beans, but the cooks will substitute fries if you ask. And the full lunch menu is offered until 10 PM. Sushi is served during the off-season on Wednesday nights, and the place usually is packed with locals. Desserts are creamy, delicious and change daily. Some of our favorites are turtle cheesecake and Tortuga's gargantuan chocolate chip cookies.

There's a full bar here with loads of speciality drinks. We also enjoy the Black and Tans, a combination of Bass Ale and Guinness, poured to almost overflowing in pint-sized glasses. If you're a beer lover and haven't discovered this duo yet, be sure to order one on your next trip to Tortuga's (see our Nightlife chapter). This hip, laid-back eatery is open seven days a week for lunch and dinner from late February through December. Call for winter hours.

Pier House Restaurant

$ • Nags Head Fishing Pier, N.C. Hwy. 12, MP 11½, Nags Head • (252) 441-5141

Offering an amazing ocean view on the beach, this family-style restaurant allows patrons to sit right above the ocean. You can feel the salt spray if you dine on the screened porch, and even inside the air-conditioned building, waves sometimes crash beneath the wooden floor's slats. This is a great, laid-back place to enjoy a big breakfast before a day of fishing or to take a break from angling on a hot afternoon. The staff is friendly, and all three meals of the day are traditionally prepared. Lunch includes sandwiches, soups and seafood specials. All-you-can-eat dinners also are popular picks. Each entree comes with coleslaw, hush puppies and french fries or baked potato. You can have your fish grilled, broiled or fried, and if you clean the fish you catch, the folks here will cook it for you. Appetizers and desserts also are available. Free sightseeing passes come with supper so you can stroll along the long pier after your meal and watch the anglers and surfers. Pier House Restaurant is open seven days a week from March through November. Dinner is served during summer only.

The Wharf

$$ • N.C. Hwy. 12, MP 11½, Nags Head • (252) 441-7457

You can't miss this popular beach restaurant across from the Atlantic: It's the one with the long, long line of people out front. Folks arrive early for the ever-popular all-you-can-eat seafood buffet of Alaskan crab legs, fried shrimp, scallops, chowder, broiled catch of the day, clam strips, barbecue, prime rib, homemade yeast rolls, loads of vegetables and desserts — all for less than $15.95 a person. The atmosphere is very informal. A new $4.95 children's menu offers hamburgers, hot dogs, pizza, chicken tenders, a drink and all-you-can-eat dessert served on a souvenir Frisbee. Kids 3 and younger eat for free. The Wharf is open from Easter through October. Doors open at 4 PM during the summer. The Wharf is closed Sundays. Alcoholic beverages are not served here.

Seafare Restaurant

$$ • U.S. Hwy. 158, MP 13½, Nags Head • (252) 441-5555

So how does one of the oldest and most successful of the array of seafood buffet places on the Outer Banks celebrate its 45th birthday? How about by cutting prices. The folks at Seafare have shaved about $4 off the buffet menu prices that were in effect during 1997.

For a restaurant that considers its tradition one of its strongest selling points, there are plenty of new things in store for 1998 at Seafare. The restaurant's backbone of a buffet returns with the crab legs and steamed shrimp, clams, mussels, crabs and scallops. The dinner menu has been expanded and — as might be expected with the arrival of new chef Lou Petrozza, formerly of the popular Italian deli of the same name in Kill Devil Hills — includes special new creations that feature fresh pasta and Italian recipes.

The rum dinner rolls and she-crab soup are still here, but they are joined with a "breads du jour" option, a yummy spinach salad with warm bacon dressing, and the new Nag's Head Clam Bake feature (with clams, mussels, shrimp, corn on the cob and all the other stuff you'd want to include at one of your own).

Seafare has a small bar with complete service. Dinner is served nightly from March through November. Reservations are not necessary, and the restaurant's outdoor playground helps keep the kids occupied while you wait for a table (remember, this place gets packed during summer). Ask about children's and senior discounts.

Penguin Isle Soundside Grille

$$$ • U.S. Hwy. 158, MP 16, Nags Head • (252) 441-2637

As night falls, waterfowl begin fluttering across the low-lying marshlands of Roanoke Sound, right outside the windows of this elegant soundside restaurant. Windsurfers in the distance cruise by beneath colorful sails, and brilliant sunsets abound. The sights outside the dining room are as lovely and tranquil as the ambiance inside. Penguin Isle is truly a peaceful place to enjoy a relaxing, intimate meal.

Here, the decor is tasteful and creative, with displays of local art, hand-carved decoys, lighted authentic ship models, enormous mounted wine bottles and light wood accents around the airy dining room. White linen tablecloths cover every table, and the lights and slow jazz music are soft and low.

Not only a premier place to dine, Penguin Isle is also a wine destination. The staff is very knowledgeable, and the much-heralded Wine Spectator's Award of Excellence identified this restaurant's wine list as "one of the best in the world" for the past six years. Seasonal wine dinners also are offered in the off-season with advance registration.

A separate window-walled lounge with full bar, an abbreviated menu and small tables overlooks the sound. Patrons can also have a cocktail before dinner on the outdoor deck, and a lobby with comfortable couches affords an alternative place to await your table. Owners Doug Tutwiler and Mike Kelly combine their talents here to create a truly distinctive restaurant. Chef Lee Miller is one of only a handful of certified working chefs on the Outer Banks, and all the staff are friendly and professional.

Penguin Isle serves fresh local seafood, handmade pasta, certified Black Angus beef, chicken, duck, fresh-baked breads and many other appetizing offerings. Creative food pairings, also called fusion cookery, is the chef's specialty, but the seafood trio platter featuring fresh fish, shrimp and scallops is hard to beat. We also recommend grilled Gulf Stream tuna over homemade fettuccine. The seafood gumbo and bean cakes are also delicious for starters here. Penguin Isle's portions are generous, especially for such an upscale restaurant. All the desserts, of course, are delectable.

Only dinner is served here from March through January. Employees also will cater private parties, wedding receptions and almost any occasion on-site. A children's menu is available, and early dining specials are offered from 5 until 6 PM.

The Dunes
$ • U.S. Hwy. 158, MP 16½, Nags Head • (252) 441-1600

When a large crowd or big family is gathering for a meal, this 16-year-old restaurant can accommodate everyone in its three huge dining rooms. Breakfast at The Dunes is a locals' favorite — you can tell by the packed parking lot — where every early morning entree in every imaginable combination is offered. There's also a popular breakfast bar here during weekends in the off-season and daily in the summer. Lunches include great burgers and homemade crab cakes served with fries and coleslaw. The rib-eye steak sandwich is also a good choice.

Dinners feature local, well-prepared seafood at moderate prices and a huge salad bar. All-you-can-eat specials are selected often. There are also plenty of desserts to choose from, if you're not already too full. The Dunes serves beer and wine and has a children's menu for small fries. The service is fast and friendly. The restaurant is open from mid-February through Thanksgiving seven days a week in-season (call for winter hours).

Owens' Restaurant
$$$ • N.C. Hwy. 12, MP 16½, Nags Head • (252) 441-7309

The oldest Outer Banks restaurant owned and operated continuously by the same family, Owens' is a local legend. In 1996 this upscale eatery celebrated its 50th anniversary, marking a half-century of good food and good service, which are well-appreciated by loyal patrons who return year after year.

Clara and Bob Owens first owned a small hot dog stand in Manteo. In 1946 they opened a 50-seat cafe in Nags Head on the deserted strip of sand that's now filled with hotels, rental cottages and thousands of vacationers who arrive each summer. The Owens raised their two children, Bobby and Clara Mae, in the restaurant serving breakfast, lunch and dinner during those early days. Today, Clara Mae and her husband, Lionel, run the family restaurant. R.V., Clara Mae's nephew, owns a restaurant by the same name on the Nags Head-Manteo Causeway. Clara Mae's daughter, Clara, runs a self-titled eatery on the Manteo waterfront. Together, this food-loving family serves some of the best traditional Outer Banks-style seafood on the beach.

Owens' Restaurant now seats more than 200 people and offers only evening meals. More than 90,000 dinners are served from this Beach Road eatery each season. The atmosphere is still homey, the food is still fresh and homemade, and the large lobby overflows with memorabilia of the barrier islands' and Owens family heritage. Even the building's architecture is reminiscent of the Outer Banks' past, patterned after an old Nags Head lifesaving station. The menu, however, combines modern tastes with traditional recipes. Owens' renowned Southern Thanksgiving buffet is worth experiencing just to sample the range of delights this restaurant is capable of creating.

Locally caught seafood, often fresh off the boat, is broiled, fried, sauteed or grilled each evening. Coconut shrimp, "Miss O" crab cakes and pasta are among the most popular entrees. There's a mixed grill for patrons who prefer prime rib with their fish. Live Maine lobsters, picked from the tank, are steamed just before they're placed on your plate. Homemade soups, including Hatteras-style clam chowder and lobster bisque, are delicious ways to start a meal. All of the homemade desserts are well-worth saving room for.

There's a full bar upstairs in the Station Keepers' Lounge where beer, wine, mixed drinks and special coffee concoctions are available. Light fare is also available upstairs. Owens' is open from mid-March through New Year's Eve. Dinner is served seven days a week.

Sam & Omie's
$$ • N.C. Hwy. 12, MP 16½, Nags Head • (252) 441-7366

Begun as a place for early morning anglers to indulge in a big breakfast before the Oregon Inlet charter fishing fleet took off, Sam & Omie's is one of the oldest family restaurants on the barrier islands. In fact, the famed Lost Colony production and Sam & Omie's both celebrated their 60th anniversary in 1997. Omie Tillett recently retired his boat The Sportsman, and he long ago sold this little wooden building at Whalebone Junction. The restaurant, however, retains its old beach charm and still serves hearty, homemade food cooked with traditional local recipes for breakfast, lunch and dinner.

This is a very casual place with wooden booths and tables and a full-service bar. Local fishermen congregate to contemplate the day's catch, and families flock to enjoy the low-priced, filling meals. Photographs of famous Gulf Stream catches line the walls, and the TV usually is tuned in to some exciting sporting event. For breakfast, omelettes are our favorite option. We like to make a meal of the rich she-crab soup and red chile poppers for lunch. Salads, sandwiches, hamburgers, fish fillets, turkey clubs and daily specials also are served. A steamer was added in 1998 for healthy steamed vegetables and fish. For dinner, try a soft-shell crab sandwich in-season or a prime rib entree on Thursdays. Sam & Omie's is open from early March through December, at least. Call for winter hours.

Jennette's Pier Restaurant & Pub
$$ • N.C. Hwy. 12, MP 16½, Nags Head • (252) 480-6600

Entering its second season in 1998, Jennette's bills itself as "the restaurant with the million dollar view." No argument there — diners can look out one of the restaurant's many windows and see 5 miles north up the beach. Stormy weather dramatizes the view even more, with waves crashing up around the pier.

For breakfast, try eggs served with catfish, herring roe, steak or sausage, grilled ham or bacon. Eggs Benedict, omelettes and Belgian waffles are other offerings. Lunch items include sandwiches options like fried flounder, soft shell crab, grilled Cajun chicken and Reubens. Hot plates and baskets — clam strips, oysters, shrimp or scallops, grilled pork chops — are also available, in addition to an interesting selection of appetizers. Dinners include prime rib, broiled and fried seafood platters, crab cakes, lobster tail, chicken, steak and pasta. A children's menu is available.

Specialty drinks and kiddie cocktails are offered from the pub. There is a also a "pub grub" menu with light fare including veggie burgers, barbecue sandwiches, crab cakes, hot wings, chips and salsa, mozzarella sticks, she-crab soup and steamed shrimp. Jennette's serves three meals a day in-season. Hours are 6 AM to 9 PM. Pub grub is available from noon to 11:30 PM.

RV's
$$ • Nags Head/Manteo Cswy., Nags Head • (252) 441-4963

Celebrating its 16th year this summer, RV's is one of the most popular places on the beach for lunch and dinner. Just check the parking lot if you don't believe us. Owner R.V. Owens often stops by your table to greet you, offering his warm smile, a firm handshake and maybe an opinion or two as an appetizer to an abundant meal. You can eat at the full-service bar in this casual restaurant or sit at a table in one of the soundfront dining rooms. The seafood stew is extremely tasty and filled to overflowing with shrimp and scallops. Marinated tuna is a must for fish lovers. There's also a gazebo raw bar on an attached deck overlooking the water that takes on a life of its own in the evening. Prices here are really reasonable, and the atmosphere is lively and fun. RV's is open from mid-February through Thanksgiving seven days a week.

Tale of the Whale
$$ • Nags Head/Manteo Cswy., Nags Head • (252) 441-7332

Family-operated and owned for 20 years, Tale of the Whale is situated right on the Roanoke Sound. You can enjoy the delightful views either looking through the expansive windows inside while savoring dinner, or out on the 75-foot deck and gazebo while sipping a refreshing cocktail. Newly decorated, this roomy establishment is bright and airy, with big wooden booths lining the walls. Tables fill out the center of the two dining rooms, and a 40-foot bar is on the north side where diners can watch sunsets and bird life dance on the water.

Tale of the Whale serves a variety of the freshest available food in generous portions. Seafood, lots of pasta, steaks and prime rib are staples of the menu. Specials, featuring everything from a mixed grill to broiled shellfish, are offered daily, and early-bird specials are available from 4 to 5 PM. Combination platters can be served fried or broiled. Desserts are homemade and baked on the premises. Tale of the Whale is open daily for dinner from April through October.

Basnight's Lone Cedar Cafe
$$ • Nags Head/Manteo Cswy., Nags Head • (252) 441-5405

One of the newer Outer Banks restaurants, Lone Cedar Cafe opened in the spring of 1996 to serve lunch and dinner. The Basnight family of Manteo operates this casual, upscale eatery where diners wearing everything from shorts to suits are welcome. In fact, it's not unusual to see the president pro tem of the state senate himself, Marc Basnight, talking with guests and removing dinner plates. Checkered green-and-white tablecloths cover every table. You'll notice the hunting motif with duck decoys and fishing memorabilia in honor of the former barrier island hunt club for which the eatery is named.

Appetizers are plentiful, ranging from onion straws to clam chowder, seafood bisque, clam and oyster fritters, hot crab balls and hot crab dip plus soups and other specials of the day. Lunch entrees start at $3.95 and include sandwiches and fresh local seafood. For dinner try black Angus beef, homemade pasta, sliced duck breast or fried or broiled seafood or order any of the evening specials. Each meal is accompanied by a salad, choice of potato, rolls and homemade corn bread. There's a full bar and an extensive wine list here. Desserts, home-baked daily, include pumpkin and pecan praline cheesecakes; pecan, peanut butter, lemon or Key lime pie; banana fritters and Lebanese chocolate cake.

This cafe offers a view of the water from every table and is open for lunch and dinner daily year round. Vegetarian and children's offerings are available. Reservations are not accepted.

The Oasis
$$ • Nags Head/Manteo Cswy., Nags Head • (252) 441-7721

This waterfront building was constructed as a restaurant in the 1940s, making it one of the oldest continuously operated eateries on the beach. Violet Kellam bought the building in 1950, and her grandchildren, Mike, Mark and Kellam France, took the place over several years ago. Framed black-and-white photographs of barefoot 1950s-era waitresses still flank the walls.

Open for breakfast, lunch and dinner April through Christmas, this restaurant offers a panoramic view of the sound. Breakfast includes traditional eggs, bacon and pancake options. Fresh seafood and hearty sandwiches are served for lunch. For dinner try a daily special or featured entree such as peppered salmon, blackened tuna or prime rib. The steam bar serves oysters, shrimp, clams, crab legs and live lobsters. The Oasis has a children's menu, and full bar service is available evenings. Diners coming by boat can tie up at the new 200-foot dock. Before or after a meal, patrons can stroll along the 100-foot pier or sit and admire the view from the 500-square-foot gazebo. Acoustic entertainment is offered in the summer.

Roanoke Island

Manteo

The Weeping Radish Brewery & Bavarian Restaurant
$$ • U.S. Hwy. 64, Manteo • (252) 473-1157

Next to the Christmas Shop on the main highway in Manteo, this large Bavarian restaurant includes an outdoor beer garden, separate pub, children's playground and two-story dining room. A European flavor prevails throughout. Traditional German meals include veal, sauerbraten and a variety of sausages. Homemade noodles, also called spaetzle, and cooked red cabbage are flavorful side dishes offering unusual tastes you won't find elsewhere on the Outer Banks. Continental cuisine also is available.

The restaurant's name comes from the radish served in Bavaria as an accompaniment to beer. Cut in a spiral, it's sprinkled with salt and packed back together. The salt draws out the moisture and gives the radish the appearance of weeping. Beer isn't served with radishes here (except by special request), but the brews are certainly the best part about this place. A microbrewery opened at The Weeping Radish in 1986 offering pure, fresh handcrafted German beer without chemical additives or preservatives. You can watch this "nectar of the gods" being brewed on-site. Take home an extra pint to enjoy later. The Weeping Radish is open all year seven days a week for lunch and dinner.

Garden Deli & Pizzeria
$, no credit cards • U.S. Hwy. 64, Manteo • (252) 473-6888

Shaded by pine trees, this tiny restaurant has a breezy outdoor deck perfect for summer dining. The cheerful, hometown crew at the eatery have watched their Garden grow into one of the most popular lunch spots for the working crowd in Manteo. Here, New York-style pizzas are cooked to order and packaged to go, if you wish. White pizza, one of our favorites, is topped with ricotta, mozzarella, Parmesan and Romano cheeses, broccoli and minced garlic. Traditional red sauce pizzas and specialty pizzas also are offered. The Philly cheese steaks, burgers, gyros and a wide assortment of deli sandwiches, homemade salads and antipasto salads are wonderful. Fresh tuna and chicken salad plates are just right for a light lunch or dinner.

For breakfast, bagels, muffins and sandwiches are available. Garden Pizzeria offers free evening delivery to Roanoke Island and Pirate's Cove. The restaurant is open for breakfast, lunch and dinner Monday through Saturday year round. Garden also offers catering.

Big Al's Soda Fountain & Grill

$ • U.S. Hwy. 64, Manteo • (252) 473-5570

You can't miss Big Al's, across from the Christmas Shop in downtown Manteo. The talk of the town since construction began the winter of 1996-97, locals anxiously awaited the early summer opening of this down-home eatery in the huge brand-new building. Owners Vanessa and Allan Foreman were originally planning to open a little ice cream parlor, but the concept expanded into a full-blown soda fountain and family restaurant. It's definitely a place to take the kids. With '50s decor and memorabilia, Big Al's is a great place to kick back and enjoy some good ol' American food and fountain treats. Plus, you can get fish so fresh, it's literally off-the-boat, says Vanessa. She should know because Allan catches most of it.

Children's meals are available for $2.95. Kids can also check out the game room, with a pinball machine, video games and a jukebox. There's even a dance floor. Big Al's serves lunch and dinner daily.

Darrell's Restaurant

$$ • U.S. Hwy. 64, Manteo • (252) 473-5366

This down-home restaurant started as an ice cream stand more than 30 years ago and has been a favorite family-style eatery for the past two decades. It's common knowledge that Darrell's fried oysters are among the best in town. Menu items such as popcorn shrimp, crab cakes, grilled marinated tuna and fried scallops are teamed with french fries, coleslaw and hush puppies to provide more than enough to fuel you through the day. Soups such as Dare County-style clam chowder and oyster stew are hard to resist. Salads, sandwiches and steamed and raw seafood are additional options for the hungry diner. Meat-eaters will be satiated by offerings such as delmonico steak, barbecued minced pork and grilled marinated chicken. Daily seafood specials are served for dinner; a children's and light-eater's menu is available. The hot fudge cake is a must for dessert. Beer and wine are served. Darrell's is open for lunch and dinner year round but is closed Sundays.

Clara's Seafood Grill and Steam Bar

$$$ • The Waterfront Shops, Manteo • (252) 473-1727

Overlooking Shallowbag Bay and the state ship, *Elizabeth II*, this is one of our favorite Manteo eateries where diners can watch boats on the water and see birds diving for fish. A casual, relaxing restaurant with good service and equally admirable food, Clara's lunch menu has delicious sandwiches and salads, hot soups and an ever-changing specials board. We order the black beans and rice most frequently. All the dinners are excellent, especially the mixed grill of shrimp and shrimp kebabs, filet mignon and tuna. The she-crab soup, tuna kebabs and mixed grill are some other favorites at this classy establishment. Grilled fish specials are offered every day. Caesar salads are a cool alternative on warm summer evenings. And the steam bar showcases local seafood of all sorts.

Historic photos lining the walls will remind you of what Manteo's waterfront looked like in the early days. Since this restaurant is less than a 10-minute drive from The Lost Colony amphitheater, it's a good place to take in an early meal before the outdoor drama begins. Beer, wine and champagne are available, and brown bagging is allowed. A children's menu is provided. Lunch and dinner are served here March through December.

Full Moon Cafe

$$ • The Waterfront Shops, Manteo • (252) 473-MOON

A cozy cafe overlooking Shallowbag Bay from its second-story vantage point, this eclectic eatery opened in late 1995 and consistently overflows with local and visiting patrons. Tablecloths line every table, and a plate glass window wall opens onto the water. The innovative cuisine here has a nouveau American flair. Most of the entrees and specials (which usually involve creative takes on pasta and seafood) are so unusual we haven't seen them anywhere else on the Outer Banks.

Hummus spread, baked brie and mushroom caps stuffed with shrimp are succulent appetizers. Lunch specials include gourmet sandwiches to satisfy everyone's tastes, vegetarian offerings, seafood, chicken and homemade soups, such as Hungarian mushroom, curried spinach and spicy tomato. Each entree is served with corn chips and Full Moon's own salsa. A separate dinner menu offers enticing seafood dishes, stuffed chicken breasts, roasted eggplant with other vegetables smothered in marinara sauce and provolone cheese, and beef Charron covered in Portobello mushrooms and a Gorgonzola cheese sauce. All the desserts are delightful. Beer (including some microbrews) and a good selection of wines are available. You can eat inside the lovely little dining room, dine outdoors in the courtyard or take any meal to go. Reservations are accepted for parties of six or more.

Full Moon is open for lunch and dinner seven days a week in summer. Hours are more limited in the off-season, so call for specific schedules.

Poor Richard's Sandwich Shop
$, no credit cards • The Waterfront, Manteo • (252) 473-3333

One of Manteo's favorite downtown eateries, Poor Richard's changed ownership in 1998. But new owner Tod Clissold is not about to alter the easy charm and delicious food at this waterfront establishment. With half the work force in Manteo making a bull's-eye to Poor Richard's every day, this casual eatery is a local gathering spot that's reasonably priced with fast counter service and interesting offerings. Try the cucumber sandwich with cream cheese — a cool meal that surprises your palate. Sandwiches are made-to-order, and specials are offered daily. Soups, meatless chili, hot dogs, salad plates, cookies and ice cream are also available. Breakfast includes scrambled egg and bacon sandwiches, bagels and cream cheese and fresh fruit. Steamed shrimp is available for lunch and dinner.

Whatever your mode of transportation — boat, bike, car or legs — Poor Richard's is a worthy fueling station. You can eat inside at a roomy booth or take your meal out on the back porch and enjoy the waterfront view — there always seems to be enough room for everybody. Poor Richard's is open daily in the summer for breakfast, lunch and dinner. Call for off-season hours.

1587
$$$ • Tranquil House Inn, Queen Elizabeth St., Manteo • (252) 473-1587

The owner of this critically acclaimed restaurant makes your mouth water just by reading his menu aloud. The offerings are unusual, extremely upscale cosmopolitan and some of the most ambitious of any Outer Banks establishment. Ambiance is elegant and romantic: the soft glow of intimate lighting, a gleaming copper-topped bar in a separate lounge area and polished wood and mirrors that reflect the lights sparkling off boats anchored in Shallowbag Bay. Executive Chef Donny King creates a constantly changing menu that's always as fresh and fabulous as the food.

Homemade soups prepared each day include Mediterranean mussels and crayfish with spring vegetables and feta cheese in a light tomato broth. For appetizers, select sesame-encrusted colossal scallops with spicy vegetable slaw and soy-wasabi cream or grilled Portobello mushroom on a zucchini podium with balsamic-sauteed julienne vegetables. Salads, served à la carte, offer Boston Bibb, romaine and baby lettuce leaves with spring vegetables and herb-shallot vinaigrette.

Dinner entrees, each of which is an artistic masterpiece, range from crispy cornmeal rockfish with Louisiana-style crayfish butter sauce and chile-fried rice to an ocean panache of tiger prawns, mussels, scallops and fish tossed with vegetables and orzo pasta, finished with feta cheese. Another excellent choice is grilled filet mignon fanned with roasted garlic mashed potatoes and a wild mushroom and goat's cheese and Cabernet Ragout.

A children's menu offers simpler dishes for younger tastes. Vegetarian requests are welcome. The exquisite dessert creations are well worth saving room for, and are so beautiful that you may want to take a snapshot before digging in!

Named for the first year English colonists attempted to settle on Roanoke Island, 1587 serves a wide selection of wine and beer and permits brown bagging. This outstanding restaurant is open for dinner daily in the summer. Call for off-season hours. Reservations are requested.

Anna Livia's Restaurant
$$ • The Elizabethan Inn, U.S. Hwy. 64, Manteo • (252) 473-3753

Opened in 1995, this restaurant has earned acclaim for its moderately priced, contemporary and traditional Italian cuisine and generous selection of seafood. Anna Livia's features a gourmet seasonal menu and nightly specials including chicken and ravioli with mushrooms in balsamic sauce; and veal caprese sauteed with tomatoes and mozzarella cheese with basil. Pasta and chicken also are served. The lunch menu offers daily specials, sandwiches and seasonal fresh salads. Desserts are homemade, and beer and wine are served. A variety of breakfast entrees and a weekend breakfast buffet also are available. Other features include a children's menu, seniors' discounts, and a completely smoke-free environment. A full carry-out menu is available. Banquet rooms are reserved for private parties. Anna Livia's is open daily year round; on Saturday, breakfast and dinner only are served. Call for winter hours.

Wanchese

Queen Anne's Revenge
$$ • Old Wharf Rd., Wanchese • (252) 473-5466

Named after one of Blackbeard's famous pirate ships that plied the waters off Carolina's coast during the early 1700s, Queen Anne's Revenge is snuggled in a grove of trees in the scenic fishing village of Wanchese. It's one of our favorite Outer Banks restaurants, well off the beaten path at the end of a winding lane. Wayne and Nancy Gray have operated this outstanding restaurant since 1978. They use only quality ingredients, and their attention to detail really shows.

The restaurant has three dining rooms, one with a fireplace that provides a cozy ambiance during cold winter months. A large selection of appetizers is offered, including bouillabaisse (chock-full of fresh seafood) and black bean and she-crab soups. All the seafood here is excellent, from Blackbeard's Raving to the locally landed

Photo: Courtesy of Bob Reardon

You can sample fresh fish from these waters in many area restaurants.

shellfish and fish served with the Wanchese platter. There's even Châteaubriand for two, carved at your table. Queen Anne's chefs make their own pasta; in fact, their fettuccine is a staple around Wanchese. All the desserts are homemade and served in generous portions. This lovely restaurant offers a children's menu and a nice selection of beer and wine. The dining room serves dinner only seven days a week during the summer. Enjoy the Sunday lunch buffet from October through May. Queen Anne's is open all year, closing Tuesdays during the off-season.

Fisherman's Wharf
$$ • N.C. Hwy. 345, Wanchese • (252) 473-5205

Overlooking the fishing port of Wanchese, the dining room of this family-owned restaurant offers the best views around of the Outer Banks' commercial fishing fleet. Windows form an entire wall of the dining room, so diners can see the seafood they might be served this evening being unloaded from the boats in the afternoon. The fish here is as fresh and local as it gets.

The Daniels family, of Wanchese fishing history fame, opens this restaurant for lunch and dinner from late March through November. Seafood plates complete with homemade hush puppies and good coleslaw are the best selections from a variety of items on the menu. There's a grill, and landlubbers can order pasta and chicken entrees. Diners can enjoy oysters on the half shell as an appetizer. You'll want to save room for the homemade desserts. This is a casual eatery where families feel right at home. A children's menu is available. Fisherman's Wharf is closed Sundays.

Hatteras Island

Rodanthe, Waves and Salvo

Down Under Restaurant & Lounge
$$ • Rodanthe Pier, off N.C. Hwy. 12, Rodanthe • (252) 987-2277

Ocean views are spectacular at this Australian-style restaurant, perched high over the pilings of Rodanthe's pier. You can sit at the bar in this warm and friendly eatery and watch the sun set over the sound, or you can enjoy your meal in the dining room and see the pelicans glide over Atlantic waves or the moon rise over the dark sea. Decorated with authentic Australian art and memorabilia, Down Under is a one-of-a-kind on the Outer Banks. Here, you'll find crabmeat and Western omelettes for breakfast. Lunch specialties include the Great Australian bite, similar to an Aussie burger, made with hamburger, a fried egg, grilled onions, cheese and bacon. Spicy fish burgers, vegemite sandwiches and marinated chicken sandwiches are good authentic options too. Kangaroo, a delicious meat that is very popular at Down Under, is imported from Australia for 'roo stew, 'roo burgers and kangaroo curry. And you've got to try stuffed jalapenos served with Down Under's famous sweet chile sauce.

Dinner selections include Down Under shrimp stuffed with jalapeno peppers and cream cheese wrapped in bacon. We also enjoy a side order of the foot-high onion rings and a Foster's lager or Cooper's Stout. Happy hour is from 3 to 6 PM daily. Steamed, spiced shrimp are 10¢ each. Parents will appreciate the children's menu, and kids will appreciate the extraordinary decor. Everyone will enjoy the view. Down Under is open seven days a week for breakfast, lunch and dinner from April through November. The restaurant is handicapped-accessible. Reservations are recommended.

Avon

The Barefoot Pub
$$ • N.C. Hwy. 12, Avon • (252) 995-6159

Local artwork lines the walls of this quaint and comfortable bistro with the beautiful curved oak bar and tasteful, casual decor. Starting his third season in Avon, owner/operator Kevin Carmichael wanted to design a gathering place that had character and informality with a touch of class. This rustic eatery and tavern is welcoming to both tourists and locals alike. The Barefoot Pub's food offerings are upscale, and mostly revolve around whatever fresh fish is in-season. A raw bar, sandwiches, crab cakes, fried shrimp and stone oven pizzas are also available. A wide variety of microbrewed beers and tap beer — Guinness, Bass, Foster, Pete's Wicked Ale — are yours for the asking. Tap beers are even rotated seasonally. Port wine is also sold by the glass. The pub is open April through December. Lunch and dinner is served daily in the summer.

The Mad Crabber Restaurant & Shellfish Bar
$$ • N.C. Hwy. 12, Avon • (252) 995-5959

This lively place offers dinner nightly from April through November. It's not a fancy restaurant, but you'll find good, fresh seafood here and reasonable prices. It's a recipe for success that keeps people coming back — during summer the Mad Crabber usually is extremely busy. Steamed crabs and shrimp lead the way on the menu. Locally caught blue crabs, snow crabs, Dungeness crabs from the Pacific Northwest and Alaskan king crabs also are on hand. Of course, delicious crab cakes are the speciality.

If you're not feeling "crabby," try a pasta dish, the vegetarian platter or — for meat-lovers — a thick burger or juicy steak. And you must try the famous "mad platters," a pizza pie plate overflowing with crab legs, shrimp, oysters, crawdads, clams, scallops, mussels and, if requested, blue crab. All-you-can-eat specials are served on "Fat Tuesdays," along with $1 draft beers. Wine also is available. There's a special menu just for kids. A separate game room attached to the Mad Crabber has two pool tables for low-key fun.

Buxton

Diamond Shoals Restaurant
$$ • N.C. Hwy. 12, Buxton • (252) 995-5217

The parking lot at this eatery, which is within walking distance of several Buxton motels, always seems to be crowded around breakfast time. Here you'll find one of the best breakfasts on Hatteras Island, featuring all your early morning favorites. Diamond Shoals is closed for lunch; dinner offerings include plenty of seafood choices, featuring fried and broiled seafood and some good nightly specials. Steaks and other landlubber specials are also available.

In 1998 the owner added a remarkable new 200-gallon saltwater aquarium stocked with tropical and Gulf Stream sea life. Diners can get a close-up look at corals, anemones and a variety of fascinating marine creatures. Diamond Shoals is open March through December.

Orange Blossom Cafe and Bakery
$$, no credit cards • N.C. Hwy. 12, Buxton • (252) 995-4109

Henry and Michel Schliff started Papagayo's Restaurant in Chapel Hill in 1978, and then relocated to Buxton where they opened the

Orange Blossom. Now in its seventh year, this wonderful cafe serves great Mexican cuisine on Hatteras. The sandwiches made with thick, homemade Italian bread always are a good bet. This little spot also caters to vegetarians, serving a wide selection of meatless salads, sandwiches and entrees. The Orange Blossom starts the day offering an array of baked goods and keeps serving until mid-afternoon. The famous Apple Uglies, huge apple fritter-style pastries piled high with fruit, are our favorite early morning treats. This restaurant is open daily from 7 AM until 2 PM year round, except for December 15 through January 15, for take-out or eat-in.

Billy's Fish House Restaurant
$$ • N.C. Hwy. 12, Buxton • (252) 995-5151

Can you tell that this always-bustling eatery occupies a former fish house? If the simple wooden architecture and wharf-front location didn't give it away, you might notice something fishy when you glimpse down and see the slanted concrete floors sloped for easy washing so the fish scales could flow back into the sound. Billy's is now a down-home restaurant where everything is casual and easy-going. It also serves some of the best Outer Banks seafood prepared with traditional, local recipes. The tilefish is a popular choice, and we highly recommend the homemade crab cakes. All the seafood is fresh. Each entree comes with your choice of vegetables and hush puppies. Most of the foods are lightly fried with peanut oil (except the new pasta offerings, of course). And everything is served on disposable plates with plastic utensils. Billy's is open for lunch and dinner daily from early April through mid-November.

Frisco

Bubba's Bar-B-Q
$ • N.C. Hwy. 12, Frisco • (252) 995-5421

If you're in the mood for some genuine Carolina barbecue, you won't be able to miss Bubba's — just follow your nose to this famous roadside joint. The hickory fires start early here so the pork, chicken, beef, ribs and turkey can cook slowly over an open pit behind the counter. The late Larry "Bubba" Schauer and his wife, Julie, brought their secret recipe from West Virginia to Hatteras Island more than a decade ago — and the food has been drawing locals and tourists to their eatery ever since. Homemade coleslaw, baked beans, french fries and corn bread round out the meal and diners' bellies.

The homemade sweet potato and coconut custard pies, cobblers and other desserts are delectable. Mrs. Bubba's Double Devil Chocolate Cake is approaching celebrity status. Bubba's has a children's menu and a nice selection of beer and soft drinks. All items are available for eating in or taking out. Bubba's Sauce is now a hot commodity with barbecue fans and is sold at retail and specialty shops across the Outer Banks. Bubba's is open daily for lunch and dinner during the summer. Call for winter hours. You'll find a second Bubba's, (252) 995-4385, farther north on N.C. 12 in Avon, near the Food Lion.

Hatteras Village

Gary's Restaurant
$$ • N.C. Hwy. 12, Hatteras Village
• (252) 986-2349

In recent years, this restaurant has grown from a fast-food style eatery to a small cafe. You can relax over a cup of coffee and a great breakfast here or enjoy a nice lunch any day of the week year round. Breakfast treats include crabmeat omelettes, Belgian waffles, steak and eggs, homemade biscuits and fresh fruit cups. For lunch, choose from steamed shrimp, clams, deli or sub sandwiches and a variety of seafood entrees.

For dinner, choose prime rib, fresh local seafood or one of the nightly specials. Homemade cheesecakes and fudge cakes are divine desserts. Beer and wine are available, and carry-out is an option for any item. A separate smoking area is set aside inside. Gary's is open for breakfast, lunch and dinner daily except Tuesdays in-season. Call for off-season hours.

The Channel Bass
$$ • N.C. Hwy. 12, Hatteras Village • (252) 986-2250

Owned by the Harrison family, well known for its fishing heritage, this canal-side restaurant has been a Hatteras Village institution for more than 30 years. You'll notice all of Mrs. Shelby Harrison's fishing trophies in the foyer. The Channel Bass has one of the largest menus on the beach, loaded with seafood platters, crab imperial crab cakes, veal and charbroiled steaks that the chefs slice in-house. An old family recipe is used for the hush puppies, and all the salad dressings are homemade. Make sure you try the homemade coconut, Key lime and chocolate cream pies. A private dining room is available, and large groups are welcome. The Channel Bass has early bird discounts and different dinner specials every night. A nice selection of beer and wine is served; brown bagging is allowed. A children's menu is available. Dinner is served seven days a week from mid-March through November.

Breakwater Island Restaurant
$$ • N.C. Hwy. 12, Hatteras Village • (252) 986-2733

If dining in a comfortable atmosphere with a stunning view of Pamlico Sound or relaxing with some live music on a deck at sunset sounds good, then this restaurant is the place for you. Here, a second-story dining room, deck and bar overlook a small harbor and stone breakwater, providing a unique feel to this locally loved outpost.

The dinner menu features fresh, progressive seafood dishes, prime rib, veal and pasta, all served in generous portions. Entrees are accompanied by a selection of vegetables, salad and fresh-baked breads. Live entertainment is performed atop the deck on summer Sunday evenings between 8 PM and midnight. Dinner is served seven days a week during the season. A good selection of beer and wine is available. Children's items are also offered. Check for winter hours.

Ocracoke Island

The Fig Tree
$, no credit cards • N.C. Hwy. 12, Ocracoke Village • (252) 928-4554

The Fig Tree, a tiny delicatessen offering carry-out cuisine only, packs picnics for ferry boat rides and serves a variety of light lunches and baked goods. Veggie pockets here are stuffed to overflowing with lettuce, tomatoes, cucumbers, carrots, mushrooms, sprouts and feta cheese and topped with a choice of homemade dressing. Shrimp and tuna salad are made with just-off-the-boat seafood. You can also design your own sandwich from numerous selections of meats and cheeses to be served on bakery-fresh bread, a hearty bagel or inside a pita. Baked delights include jumbo cinnamon rolls, doughnuts, fruit and nut breads, breakfast biscuits and gourmet cookies. Heavier dessert items, also outstanding, range from chocolate swirl cheesecake atop brownie crumb crust to Ocracoke's own fig cake, each served whole or by the slice.

The Fig Tree also makes a traditional tomato sauce and cheese pizza, a white garden pizza and a Greek tomato pie, all with homemade crusts. The Fig Tree is open March through December.

Pony Island Restaurant
$$ • N.C. Hwy. 12, Ocracoke Village• (252) 928-5701

A casual, homey place that lots of people come back to time and again, this restaurant features big breakfasts of biscuits, hotcakes, omelettes and the famous Pony Potatoes — hash browns covered with cheese, sour cream and salsa. Dinner entrees range from Chinese and Southwestern cuisine to a variety of interesting fresh seafood creations. The folks here even will cook your own catch of the day for you, as long as you've cleaned the fish first. Beer and wine are served, and homemade desserts add a great finishing touch to a tasty meal. The Pony Island Restaurant is adjacent to the Pony Island Motel. Breakfast here begins at 7 AM. The restaurant closes during lunchtime then reopens for dinner nightly from late March through November.

The Back Porch
$$$ • 1324 Country Rd., Ocracoke Village • (252) 928-6401

Whether you dine on the wide, breezy screened porch, eat in this quaint restaurant's small nooks or get seated in the open dining room of this well-respected restaurant, you'll find that dinners at the Back Porch are some of the most pleasant experiences on the Outer Banks. This older building was renovated and refurbished to blend with the many trees on the property. It's off the main road, surrounded by waist-high cacti, and is a quiet place to enjoy appealing entrees and comfortable conversation. Overall, it's one of our favorite restaurants on the 120-mile stretch of barrier islands. It's well worth the two-hour trip from Nags Head, including the free ferry ride, just to eat here.

The menu is loaded with fresh herbs, vegetables and seafood, most of which is caught nearby. All sauces, dressings, breads and desserts are made right in the restaurant's huge kitchen. And each piece of meat is hand-cut. In addition to the quality ingredients, the chefs come up with some pretty outrageous taste combinations, and all of them seem to blend perfectly. The crab cakes with red pepper sauce are outstanding. And you won't want to miss the smoked bluefish or crab beignets appetizers. Non-seafood dishes are a tasty option as well. Our favorite is the Cuban black bean and Monterey Jack cheese casserole.

Reduced prices and smaller portions are available for children and senior citizens. And all the desserts are divine. Freshly ground coffee is served here, and the wine selections and imported beers are as ambitious as the menu. If you get hooked — like we are — you can try your hand at some of the restaurant's recipes at home after buying a *Back Porch Cookbook*. Be prepared, however. Some of these menu items are quite involved. After reading the recipes you'll be even more impressed with the upscale culinary concoctions served in this laid-back island eatery. Dinner is offered nightly here in-season.

Howard's Pub & Raw Bar Restaurant

$ • N.C. Hwy. 12, Ocracoke Village • (252) 928-4441

Always a fun, friendly place to go for a meal, this year Howard's Pub has just about doubled its floor space on the first level, giving diners, drinkers and dancers room to spread out and expand their possibilities. Even the beer list has grown — in 1997, the pub increased its number of different imported and domestic brews from 175 to 214, where it still hovers.

Howard's Pub is the only Ocracoke establishment that can boast it's open an average of 365 days a year, including Christmas. Owners Buffy and Ann Warner hail from West Virginia, where he was a senator and she worked for the governor as director of economic development. Their lifestyles have changed a bit since purchasing this pub. And you can tell they love it. This is a must-stop for everyone on Ocracoke, with great local flavor and guaranteed good times (see our Nightlife chapter). You can relax on the huge — also recently doubled in size — screened-in porch that stretches the length of this long restaurant — or sit inside at a wooden table.

The restaurant is the only raw bar on the island and is the home of the spicy oyster shooter. We love these raw oyster and Tabasco combinations, especially when washed down with an unusual imported beer. Howard's appetizers range from soups and salads to jalapeno poppers and hot wings. Lunch and dinner items include subs, burgers and fish sandwiches. Snow crab legs, fried shrimp and wine by the bottle were recently added to the menu. Buffy also added a Cabernet and a Chardonnay made by private label winery Jefferson Vineyard of Charlottesville, Virginia.

Within the not-so-distant future, a new upper deck will be added as part of the restaurant's three-part expansion. The top deck will afford a view of the ocean, sound, salt marshes and sand dunes. On a clear day, you'll even be able to see Portsmouth Island! There's a wide-screen TV, several smaller ones, free popcorn and games such as chess, a Barrel of Monkeys and Trivial Pursuit to entertain. With the newly expanded dance floor, you'll have lots of room to dance to live music in the evenings. Food and drinks are served every day from lunchtime into the wee hours.

Cafe Atlantic
$$ • N.C. Hwy. 12, Ocracoke Village• (252) 928-4861

This traditional beach-style building was opened a few years ago by Bob and Ruth Toth. There's not much that's traditional about their innovative, fantastic food, however. Views from the dining room look out across marsh grass and dunes. The gallery-like effect of the restaurant is created with hand-colored photographs by local writer and artist Ann Ehringhaus.

There's a nonsmoking dining room upstairs and a smoking section downstairs. Lunch and dinner are served at this upscale yet casual eatery seven days a week in-season. And the Sunday brunches from 11 AM to 3 PM are the best we've found south of Duck. Brunch menus change weekly, but champagne and mimosas always are served. We're partial to the blueberry pecan pancakes, chicken and broccoli crepes and the huevos rancheros served over black beans in a crisp tortilla shell. Hash browns come with almost every entree. And the flavorful food will fill you up at least until supper.

The Toths make all their soups, dressings, sauces and desserts from scratch. Lunches feature a variety of sandwiches and salads. Dinner entrees include caciucco, a combination of fresh fish, shrimp, scallops and mussels in marinara sauce served over linguine; and a wide range of beef, chicken, lasagna and other excellent seafood and pasta plates fill out the menu. Each meal is served with salad, rice or potato and steaming rolls just out of the oven. You've gotta leave room for dessert here, or take one of their outrageously ornate cakes, pies or cobblers home. A children's menu is available, and the restaurant has a nice selection of wine and beer. Cafe Atlantic is open from early March through October. Lunches may vary in the off-season, so call for hours. This cafe, though isolated on tiny Ocracoke, is certainly among the best dining experiences the Outer Banks has to offer.

Ocracoke Coffee
$ • Back Rd., Ocracoke Village • (252) 928-7473

The neatest place on the island to take care of those unavoidable caffeine and sugar needs, Ocracoke Coffee has enjoyed tremendous success since opening for the 1996 season. The aromatic eatery is filled with bagels, pastries, desserts, brewed coffee drinks, espresso, shakes, whole bean coffees and loose tea. The shop is nestled under tall pines on Back Road, within an easy walk of most anything in the village. We know you'll find your way here in the morning (everyone does), but why not shuffle in after dinner for something sweet as well? The shop's feel is way hip, but it's also cozy and inviting, and the folks frothing your concoctions are friendly as can be. For 1998 the shop is expanding the smoothie menu — look for more than 10 varieties for a cool respite from the summer heat.

Ocracoke Coffee is open daily from 7 AM to 10 PM. The shop closes December through March.

Island Inn Restaurant
$$ • Lighthouse Rd., Ocracoke Village • (252) 928-7821

This family-owned and operated restaurant at the Island Inn is one of the oldest establishments on Ocracoke. Its main dining room and airy porch are furnished in a traditional country style, with blue and white china to dine on and bright, nautical touches throughout. Breakfast and dinner are served here daily except in the dead of winter. Owners Bob and Cee Touhey make sure everyone, not just Inn guests, are welcome to eat here. Standard breakfast fare, such as pancakes, eggs and hash browns, is available. The cook also comes up with some unusual creations, such as oyster omelettes with spinach and bacon, and shrimp omelettes drenched with melted Jack cheese, green chiles and salsa.

For dinner, locally landed seafood and shellfish entrees can be grilled, fried or broiled to your liking. Beef, pork, lamb, pasta and stir-fry dishes also are available, as are vegetarian offerings. All the breads and soups are made daily at this restaurant, and homemade pies are perfectly delicious. A selection of wines is served here, and a children's menu is available. Reservations are needed for large groups; the

Photo: Courtesy of Jeanne Reilly

Seafood lovers will find many delectable dishes in Outer Banks restaurants.

owners are happy to accommodate private party requests. Call for off-season hours.

Creekside Cafe
$ • N.C. Hwy. 12, Ocracoke Village • (252) 928-3606

Overlooking Silver Lake Harbor from a second-story vantage point, the views from this 4-year-old restaurant are wonderful. A covered porch around two sides of the wooden building has ceiling fans and breezes to cool afternoon diners. Inside, the eatery is casual and friendly, serving brunch items daily and lunch and dinner from a single menu between April and early November. Soups, salads, seafood and pasta dishes are the afternoon and evening fare here. The blackened chicken sandwiches are so popular that the owners decided to package and sell the spices. French dips, fresh fish sandwiches, oyster baskets, crab cakes and Greek-style linguine with feta cheese and black olives all are great choices. For brunch, we recommend the Tex-Mex: scrambled eggs, onions, peppers, tomatoes and salsa served in a tortilla shell with a dollop of guacamole. Desserts include parfaits, cheesecakes, Key lime pie, tollhouse pie and pecan pie — all homemade. Beer and wine are available, and four champagne drinks offer unusual alcoholic creations.

 *Sand Dollar Motel*

*On a secluded street, near
restaurants and shops ...
We also have an efficiency
apartment and one cottage,
all fully furnished ...
Come and enjoy our beautiful
swimming pool.
We serve a complimentary
continental breakfast
and provide pick-up service
to and from the airport
and boat docks.*

252-928-5571
P.O. Box 461
Ocracoke Island
NC 27960

*Newly owned & operated
by an Ocracoke Native*

Nightlife

You've showered off the sand and sunscreen at the end of an active day at the beach — now you're ready to sample the Outer Banks after dark.

The Outer Banks after hours aren't like other resort areas. So many families come here — and so many early-rising anglers — that many people are bedded down for the evening by 9 PM. But in-season, when the beaches are loaded with vacationers, bars and dance floors across the barrier islands are hopping. And if you're a night owl, or at least like to stretch your wings a bit on vacation, there's always fun and frolic to be found in dozens of establishments from Corolla to Ocracoke.

If what you want to do is unwind — or gear up, if that's more your style — there are plenty of places to shoot pool, catch sporting events on big-screen TVs, play interactive trivia, throw darts, listen to low-key acoustic music or boogie the night away to a rocking live band.

Local musicians play everything from blues to jazz to rock to hard-core alternative and country tunes. Outer Banks and out of town cover bands and those with original songs take the stage often during the summer season. Several nightclubs on the Outer Banks assess nominal cover charges at the door, usually ranging from $1 for dueling acoustic guitar duos to $10 or more for the national acts that grace these sands between mid-May and Labor Day. Many acoustic acts, however, can be heard for free.

If live music is what you're listening for, check *The Virginian Pilot's* weekly *Coast* magazine — available free at area grocery and convenience stores and motels — for up-to-date listings in its "Club Hoppin'" section and music scene info in the "After Dark" column. WVOD 99.1 FM and WOBR 95.3 FM give daily concert updates on evening radio broadcasts.

Alcoholic beverages are available at most Outer Banks lounges until around 2 AM. Beer and wine are offered throughout the barrier islands. In Corolla and on Colington, Roanoke, Hatteras and Ocracoke islands, it is illegal to serve mixed drinks. However, with the exception of Colington Island, ABC stores sell liquor in each of those areas. And most nightclubs on those islands do allow people to brown-bag and bring in their own alcohol for the evening. Call ahead to make sure that's OK.

Several restaurants on the Outer Banks offer late-night menus or at least raw and steamer bar food until closing. Every nightclub operator will be glad to call a cab to take you home or to your hotel or rental cottage after an evening of imbibing. Beware: The legal drinking age in North Carolina is 21, and the blood-alcohol content necessary for a drunk-driving citation is only .08. So even if you've only had a couple of cocktails, play it safe and take a taxi. They are easy to hook up with, and it's a whole lot cheaper than court costs and license problems.

Although several area restaurants offer happy hour specials and most have bars within their establishments, we've only included those eateries that are open until at least midnight in this chapter.

Corolla

Planet Corolla
TimBuck II Shopping Village, N.C. Hwy. 12 • (252) 453-4644
Live acoustic music will be on-site at this easygoing bistro every Tuesday, and for four or five nights a week in summer. Dinner is served until 10 PM, and music will continue until midnight. A wide variety of wines and microbrews are available to quench the thirst. Call directly to find out more about the musical offerings.

Duck

Barrier Island Inn Restaurant and Tavern
Duck Rd. (N.C. Hwy. 12) • (252) 261-8700
A favorite nightspot in Duck village, the tavern is upstairs, separate from the restaurant. Folks enjoy fabulous sunsets overlooking Currituck Sound and indoor recreation including a pool table, dartboard and table-top shuffleboard. There's an outdoor deck where you can stargaze until closing time, and live acoustic music or bands can be heard most summer nights.

The tavern offers interactive TV trivia nightly year round, and QB1 interactive football is fun for armchair quarterbacks — especially with the free buffalo wings the tavern serves up during fall football season. Steamed shrimp, sandwiches and pizza are available late at the bar or around tables sized to accommodate any party. Barrier Island is open seven nights a week. Call for summer entertainment schedules.

Elizabeth's Cafe & Winery
Scarborough Faire, N.C. Hwy. 12 • (252) 261-6145

Join owner Leonard Logan for late-night "Jazz in the Grotto" at one of the most romantic, classy restaurants on the Outer Banks, hands down. National jazz acts entertain in the intimate atmosphere of the restaurant's wine cellar throughout the summer. Couples, singles and their friends can enjoy the tunes while feasting on superb food from a limited late-night menu. Elizabeth's is renowned for its extensive, superior selection of wines and has won *The Wine Spectator* magazine Best of the Award of Excellence for the past seven years. French beers are also served from the bottle. Additional nights with live music may be offered in the peak season, so call for information.

Reservations are necessary, as this is a small and very popular establishment. Elizabeth's is a nonsmoking eatery, but a special cigar and cigarette section is available on the outside porch.

Fishbones Raw Bar & Restaurant
Scarborough Lane Shops, Duck Rd. (N.C. Hwy. 12) • (252) 261-6991

Opened in summer 1995, this raw bar and restaurant fast became one of Duck's most popular evening hangouts. It's open every day of the year and features a full bar with five beers on tap, 50 bottled beers from all over the world, various microbrews and a wine list. During summer, deck parties are held outdoors when the weather is good. It's a casual place to catch up on conversation with old acquaintances — or to make new ones.

Kitty Hawk

Rundown Cafe
N.C. Hwy. 12, MP 1 • (252) 255-0026

If you're looking for summertime blues and jazz — or just want to sip some frothy brews — this Caribbean-style cafe is always an exciting spot to hang out on the north end of the beach. It's a great place to relax with friends, listen to some of the best music on the

Outer Banks several nights a week or just sit a spell at the long bar. You'll be comfortable coming in here alone too. There's a rooftop deck that affords great views of the ocean and the opportunity to catch some cool breezes and conversation.

A variety of domestic and imported beers are on hand, and there is a full line of liquor (ask about the specialty rum and tequila drinks). Enjoy Guinness stout, Bass and Harp beers on tap. The steam and raw bar serves seafood and vegetables until closing. By the way, Rundown is a traditional Jamaican stew, and the decor reflects the cafe's unusual name. Call ahead for a rundown of the evening entertainment at Rundown, or just stop by and check out this happening haunt.

Frisco's
U.S. Hwy. 158, MP 4 • (252) 261-7833

A popular nightspot for locals year round, this restaurant features a large, three-sided bar and beautiful terrariums and aquariums throughout the dining area. It's open seven days a week, and karaoke gives everyone a chance to take the stage. Groups are welcome and encouraged here, and singles and couples will find a good time too. There are tables of all sizes in the lounge, and drink specials are served late into the night. There's even a wide-screen TV for sports fans. Call for entertainment schedules.

Kill Devil Hills

Chilli Peppers
U.S. Hwy. 158, MP 5 • (252) 441-8081

World fusion food with a Southwestern twist is served at this small, innovative restaurant year round. The separate bar area out front always is teeming with partying people. Live entertainment and open-mike nights are featured year round. A full bar offers fresh fruit Margaritas, a nice wine selection and dozens of domestic and imported beers seven nights a week. Bartenders also serve nonalcoholic beers and fruit smoothies that complement any meal. There's an outdoor patio if you want to sip your drinks under the stars, and steamed seafood and vegetables are served until closing.

Awful Arthur's
N.C. Hwy. 12, MP 6 • (252) 441-5955

Loud, packed with people and about as popular as it gets on the Outer Banks, this rustic restaurant features a live lobster tank and long bar downstairs and a separate upstairs lounge that affords patrons an ocean view. Locals love to hang out here, especially on Mondays when there are food and drink specials all day. Live entertainment is offered in summer. A full bar offers up lots of cold beer on tap, and raw or steamed seafood is served late into the night. The TVs always seem to be tuned to the day's most popular sporting events. The T-shirts here sell as well as the steamed shrimp. College students especially seem to enjoy Arthur's atmosphere, but people of all ages will find a good time here seven nights a week year round.

Jolly Roger Restaurant
N.C. Hwy. 12, MP 6¾ • (252) 441-6530

Adorned with hanging plants and colorful lights, the lounge at this restaurant is separate from the dining area. This is a casual place with a long, distinctive bar inlaid with seashells. There's almost always something going on here late into the night. Most summer evenings, there's live acoustic entertainment or a band. Outer Banks folk favorite Jamie Jamison plays a variety of country, rock and blues tunes every Thursday night and usually brings some musician friends with him. The Wilder Brothers perform often throughout the year, and the bar is open seven nights a week. There is also karaoke, and interactive TV, featuring games from sports to movie trivia, draws a regular audience. Prizes are even awarded to some of the big winners. Locals love this place, and you'll find people from their early 20s to late 60s hanging out here.

Sea Ranch Lounge
Quality Inn Sea Ranch, N.C. Hwy. 12, MP 7 • (252) 441-7126

A longtime tradition for Outer Banks' shaggers, this lounge in the Sea Ranch hotel features local musician Buzz Bessette Tuesday through Saturday year round. He plays a variety of dance music from the '50s to the '90s, and there's almost always someone cutting a rug on the dance floor. A full bar is open seven nights a week, and a large-screen TV is always on for added entertainment. Recorded beach music is played here on Sunday and Monday nights. Line-dance lessons and line dancing go on every Wednesday night. The low-key atmosphere seems to attract a more mature crowd than other Outer Banks establishments.

Goombay's Grille and Raw Bar
N.C. Hwy. 12, MP 7 • (252) 441-6001

This popular nightspot teems with tourists and locals year round and is open seven nights a week. It's fun and colorful with a tropical island flair and flavor — and the bartenders all are local characters. Goombay's is Caribbean and casual, the kind of hangout where you're sure to feel right at home even if you've never visited the Outer Banks.

On Wednesdays live bands play here for an increasingly crowded "Locals Night" year round — visitors make it the-more-the-merrier in summer. A horseshoe-shaped bar is set to the side of the dining area, so you can lounge on a stool or high-backed chair in the bar area or have a seat at a nearby table after the dining room closes at 10 PM. Goombay's serves lots of imported and domestic beers, wine and mixed drinks until 2 AM. Be sure to try some of the special rum, vodka and tequila combos that come with toys to take home. Steamed shrimp and veggies are served until closing.

Quagmire's
N.C. Hwy. 12, MP 8 • (252) 441-9188

"Quags," as many locals call it, is owned by the same groovy guy who runs Goombay's, so you know once you step inside or out onto one of the biggest open-air oceanfront decks on the beach, you're bound to have a great time. A horseshoe-shaped bar faces the Atlantic — everyone sitting on a stool is guaranteed a gorgeous view.

Frozen drinks are served outdoors or in, and the bartenders even pour pitchers of Margaritas so you don't have to keep getting up to fill your thin-stemmed, salt-encrusted glass. Beer, wine and mixed drinks are available, and there's a whole line of appetizers and munchies to sample through the night. Quagmire's is open seven days a week in summer, featuring live acoustic music many nights. On the sand below the bar, horseshoes, a ring toss and a beach volleyball court beckon people to come play if they need a break from partying in the lounge. Quagmire's is open daily April through October; call for the entertainment schedule.

Port O' Call Gaslight Saloon
N.C. Hwy. 12, MP 8½ • (252) 441-7484

One of the area's most unusual places to hang out — and one of the only local nightclubs that attracts national bands in summer — the Gaslight Saloon is decorated in an ornate Victorian style complete with overstuffed armchairs, antique wooden tables and a long mahogany bar. There's a nice dance floor here and an upstairs lounge (with separate bar) that overlooks the stage.

Port O' Call features live entertainment seven nights a week in-season and every weekend while the restaurant is open from mid-March through December. There's usually a cover charge here for the bigger-name bands. In recent years, Port O' Call has hosted such national acts as the ultra-hip trailer-park boogie of Southern Culture on the Skids, hirsute blues legend Leon Russell, eclectic rockers Fishbone, Southern rock cliche-mongers Molly Hatchet, and an array of first-rate reggae artists. Beer, wine and liquor are served until 2 AM.

The Pit
U.S. Hwy. 158, MP 9 • (252) 480-3128

One of the few clubs to offer entertainment for underage kids, in addition to national name acts for adults, The Pit has become wildly popular since it opened its expanded surf shop/cyberpub in 1997. Live music is offered five nights a week. Disco dance parties are held every Friday, and modern dance night is Sunday. The sound system for both live music and CDs really packs a sweet punch. Every Wednesday in summer, The Pit hosts all ages from 8 PM to 3 AM. All teens — or even younger kids if they're supervised — are welcome to dance to a combination of rave and live music. No alcohol, of course, is served.

The rest of the week, patrons can sample the wide selection of microbrews and domestic and imported beers. A neat antique Foosball table, a pool table, darts and two computer terminals providing free Internet access all night are also available here. In 1998 The Pit added a full restaurant that serves such stomach fillers as burrito wraps, tacos and appetizers. Call for weekly entertainment schedules. See our Watersports chapter for more on the surf shop operation. The Pit is open year round.

Hurricane Alley
Sea Holly Square, N.C. Hwy. 12, MP 9½ • (252) 480-3667, (252) 441-1533

Hurricane Alley immediately found its niche in summer 1997 as a hot spot on the barrier islands. Tucked away in the Sea Holly Square mall, it's a restaurant and nightspot combined, offering great food, Foosball, trivia games and three big-screen TVs. Instead of showing just the usual sports, homemade videos of regular people doing Outer Banks activities like surfing are displayed. But when something big is happening in the sports world, one of the sets will also feature those events.

A full-service pub with domestic and imported beers, three beers (one dark) on tap, a great wine selection and liquor service, Hurricane Alley features live blues, rock and alternative bands on Saturdays all winter and three to four times a week in summer. Acoustic music will also be offered. Call for an entertainment schedule. Appetizers, lasagna and Caesar salads are available until 2 AM.

Millie's Diner
N.C. Hwy. 12, MP 10 • (252) 480-3463

Since it opened in 1996, this art-deco diner has become a favorite hangout for discerning Outer Bankers looking for some good food, music and talk in a classy, relaxed atmosphere. Serving up a great selection of wine and beer at the full bar, Millie's also boasts live jazz by local favorites performed periodically on Sunday nights. Don't be deceived by the narrow appearance outside this glittering silver diner — the inside is far roomier than you'd ever guess and is decorated in appealing art deco with yellow and burgundy appointments. You can sit at the counter-type bar and enjoy your brew, or stroll to the large back dining room to watch the entertainment.

Millie's will present live bands for entertainment occasionally on weekend nights throughout the summer. Even when there's no live music, check out the eclectic selection of rhythm and blues, funk and rock on the old-fashioned jukeboxes found at the bar and in the booths. Millie's serves American and European microbrews and two high-quality beers (the selections rotate) on tap. It's open seven days a week from Easter through Labor Day. Off-season hours will vary.

Colington Island

Blue Crab Tavern
Colington Rd., 1.5 miles west of U.S. Hwy. 158 • (252) 441-5919

A favorite afternoon and evening haunt for this island's fishing enthusiasts, Blue Crab includes an indoor bar, pool tables, video games and one of the best soundfront decks in the area. Anglers often pull their boats up to the rectangular deck and tie onto the wooden pilings to sip a few beers outdoors after work. Lots of local characters hang out here, and if you sit a spell, you're sure to hear what's biting where. Liquor is not available, but brews are cold and among the cheapest you'll find. There's a horseshoe pit out front if you feel like tossing a few around after you've tossed a few down.

Nags Head

Red Drum Taphouse
N.C. Hwy. 12, MP 10, Nags Head • (252) 480-1095

One of the newest establishments on the beach, Red Drum pours 18 beers on tap — hence the name. These are no run of the mill brews — try Sierra Nevada, J.W. Dundee's Honey Brown, Woodpecker Cider, Black Radish or Pyramid Hefeweizen. All the domestics are available as well, and you can get wine by the glass or the bottle. Red Drum also serves liquor from its beautiful long redwood-colored bar.

Every Monday night in-season is open-mike night. On Thursdays local and out-of-town bands play a variety of music ranging from rock, blues and jazz to alternative. A minimum cover is charged. Beer specials are offered all night. A pool table, Foosball table and dartboard are in an adjacent bar area that's separate from the dining room. Why not try a little competition with the tunes?

The Comedy Club and Lounge at the Carolinian
N.C. Hwy. 12, MP 10 • (252) 441-7171

This is the oldest oceanfront summer comedy club in the country, featuring soon-to-be stars for more than 14 years now. Favorite TV comics Sinbad, Brett Butler and Drew Carey all tickled funny bones from this eclectically adorned stage. National comedians are booked every summer. Reservations are recommended; although the room is big, it often gets packed in season. There's a full bar here, and cocktail servers offer tableside service throughout the show. One cover charge includes three comics who always put on hilarious acts — many that demand audience participation.

Doors open at 9 PM seven nights a week in season, and the laughter begins around 10 PM. During fall and spring, the comedy club is open only on weekends. Before the show, you can enjoy your favorite beverages from a bar on the outside, oceanfront deck. The Carolinian features free live music on the deck seven evenings a week in season, weather permitting. Priority seating in the comedy club is given to those who dine in the Carolinian's restaurant, Calico Jack's.

Kelly's Tavern
U.S. Hwy. 158, MP 10 • (252) 441-4116

Probably the most consistently crowded tavern on the Outer Banks, Kelly's offers live bands six nights a week in-season and an open-mike fest with a lip-synch contest and cash prizes on the only music off-night, Tuesday. Even during fall and winter, rockin' bands take the stage, and fun people always fill this place.

A full bar serves everything from suds to shots, and folks often line up around its three long sides two or three people deep. The big dance floor is usually shaking after 10 PM. If you're in the mood just to listen and watch, secluded booths surround the dance floor a few steps above the rest of the lounge, and tables are scattered throughout the tavern. A dartboard and fireplace adorn the back area, and beach memorabilia hangs in every corner. Featuring a tasty variety of foods served late into the night, a lounge menu offers appetizers and steamed shellfish. An old-fashioned popcorn popper even provides free munchies served in wicker baskets throughout the evening. Singles seem to really enjoy this tavern.

Tortuga's Lie Shellfish Bar and Grille
N.C. Hwy. 12, MP 11 • (252) 441-7299

Our favorite place to meet friends for a laid-back evening — or to hang out alone to chat with long-lost local pals — Tortuga's offers sporadic acoustic entertainment in summer and probably the most comfortable atmosphere you'll find on the Outer Banks most of the year. Owners Richard Welch, the eatery's longtime chef, and Bob Sanders often are on hand to greet guests themselves. They renovated their restaurant a couple of years ago — regulars are now used to the closed-in porch that includes custom-made wooden booths and ceiling fans. The bar also got bigger, winding around a corner to allow at least a half-dozen more stools to slide under the refurbished countertop.

Don't worry, however, if you loved Tortuga's just as it was, you'll still find the old license plates perched on the low, wooden ceiling beams, and the sand volleyball court remains ready for pickup games out back all summer. Bartenders serve Black and Tans in those same pint glasses — that's right, Tortuga's has Guinness and Bass Ale on tap. Longneck beers are served by the bottle or by the iced-down bucket. Shooters, mixed drinks and tropical frozen concoctions are sure to please any palate.

The steamer is open until closing, so you can satisfy late-night munchies with shellfish or fresh vegetables. Whether you're new in town or here to stay, Tortuga's is one place you won't want to miss. Most nights, it remains open until 2 AM. Tortuga's closes for a brief spell in December and early January.

Sticky Wicket Pub
U.S. Hwy. 158, MP 14 • (252) 441-6594

For weeks through the winter, we Outer Banks locals were intrigued by the marquee outside the shocking pink building on the Bypass that had housed the defunct Lance's Restaurant and Bar. "Something Wicket This Way Comes," it read. That portent proved true when the nice folks that run the Sticky Wicket Pub — one of our favorite spots in the southern part of Nags Head to hoist a pint — finally moved over from their former location in the Outer Banks Mall.

The Wicket crew gutted the old building, and the result is a much larger space than they had in the mall annex. They've also painted over the sore-thumb pink to try to blend in better with the surroundings — the Wicket's exterior is now a neutral, sand color with teal trim. With all the space, the Wicket features an expanded dinner menu (more seafood, steaks and pasta dishes) to go with their old pub favorites. A big S-shaped bar is more removed from the dining area in the new building, and there will be occasional acoustic entertainment. The pub features a full bar and more beer options than you can shake a sticky wicket at. Pool, a popular pastime at the old location, looks to be an in-season casualty for space reasons, but billiards will return in the slower months.

The Sticky Wicket Pub is open daily year round for lunch and dinner. Pub food is available until 1 AM in-season.

Roanoke Island

Route 64 Cafe
U.S. Hwy. 64, Manteo • (252) 473-6081

The after-work and NASCAR crowd on Roanoke Island has found itself on Route 64 with regularity since the cafe opened under new ownership on Independence Day 1997. On the barroom side of this little pub, just across from Manteo's Chesley Mall and R.D. Sawyer's Ford dealership, you'll find a friendly staff twisting tops and serving terrific food. The selection of more than two dozen beers includes all your favorite domestics, plus a few microbrews and imports.

Pool is a popular option at Route 64, and tournaments are held on periodic Sundays. You can count on the NASCAR race (or the other big sporting event of the day) being on the tube. This is one of the few spots in Manteo for late-night munchies: Sandwiches, salads and nightly specials (the food these folks serve belies the modest look of the place) can usually be whipped up until about midnight. Route 64 is open daily year round; call for off-season operating hours.

The Green Dolphin Restaurant and Pub
Sir Walter Raleigh St., Manteo • (252) 473-5911

Acoustic entertainers perform here on Fridays year round, featuring rock, folk, blues, beach and even light jazz tunes. There's a bar serving a variety of beer, and there's never a cover charge for live music. This pub is warm and comfortable, and it's made a great comeback after a summer 1997 fire caused considerable damage and closed its heavy wooden doors for several months.

There are wooden floors, booths and tables made from old ship hatch covers and Singer sewing machine stands. The staff is friendly, and locals like to hang out here. It's a fun place with a pool table and pockmarked dartboards set in a separate room. Check out the lovely old wooden cabinet with lockers — it's a holdover from the days when folks used to brown-bag their liquor into the establishment. The restaurant serves appetizers and sandwiches late into the night. Call for seasonal schedules of entertainment.

Hatteras Island

Sandbar & Grille
N.C. Hwy. 12, Hatteras Village • (252) 986-2044

Formerly the Lightship Tavern, the Sandbar has been a hit since it opened on New Year's Eve in 1997. Even when there's no band playing at this rustic, casual establishment, you can hear a fabulous range of music on one of the 83 satellite radio channels. The station is chosen to fit the crowd — the staff says there are even a select few that do a great job clearing the house when closing time comes around.

Bands that play everything from blues and rock to jazz and alternative are featured every Friday starting at 10 PM. The cover charge is $4. On Wednesday nights a solo guitarist starts at 9 PM, and there is no cover. A pool table and Foosball are also on the premises. Call for entertainment schedules. Lunch and dinner are served all day every day. A late-night menu is available from 9 to 11 PM.

Ocracoke Island

Howard's Pub & Raw Bar Restaurant
N.C. Hwy. 12, Ocracoke Village • (252) 928-4441

Our absolute favorite place to hear live bands — featuring the friendliest crowd of locals and visitors around — Howard's Pub has an atmosphere and feeling all its own. Once you've visited, you'll plan to make at least a yearly excursion to this upbeat but laid-back place. We try to return at least once a month to get a fix of fun and to get away from it all. Howard's is open 365 days until 2 AM — the only place on the Outer Banks that can make that claim. It's also the only restaurant on Ocracoke open year round.

The pub serves more types of beer than any place we know of — at least 214 different bottles line the top shelf above the bar, showing an unusual array of offerings from around the world that are always available at this oasis on the isolated island. There's an outdoor deck here for catching sunsets or falling stars. A huge, screened porch — complete with Adirondack rocking chairs for relaxing in the evening breezes — wraps around one side of the spacious wooden building. The dance floor has more than doubled in size in recent years. A wide-screen TV offers sports fans constant entertainment, and six other TVs usually tune in to a variety of events. Howard's has a dartboard, backgammon, chess set, checkers, Trivial Pursuit, Barrel of Monkeys and card games available for free to playful patrons. Bartenders serve pizza, sandwiches and raw bar-style food until 2 AM and offer free chili Monday nights during football season.

Bands play at least three nights a week in season and can be heard here even on many winter weekends. Music ranges from rhythm and blues to bluegrass, jazz, rock and originals. Open-mike nights and karaoke are favorite events with locals and visitors alike. And the cover charge at Howard's is never more than a few dollars. Even when electricity fails the rest of the island, this pub is equipped with a generator so employees can keep on cooking — and keep the beer cold.

Jolly Roger Pub
N.C. Hwy. 12, Ocracoke Village • (252) 928-3703

A waterfront eatery overlooking Silver Lake, this pub has a huge outdoor deck that's covered in case of thunderstorms. Local entertainers often perform live acoustic music here with no cover charge. Jolly Roger serves beer, wine and finger foods throughout summer.

Attractions

Even after you've made the rounds at our most famous attractions — the beloved candy-striped Cape Hatteras Lighthouse, the world-renowned Wright Brothers National Memorial and the long-running *The Lost Colony* outdoor drama — so much more remains to be seen and done here that even natives always find new adventures every year. Attractions are available to fit every mood, age and price range.

We're not just the home of two of the most significant events in the nation's history — the first English-speaking colony and the first powered flight — we're also gifted with an extraordinary coastline. Between lighthouses, lifesaving stations, wild horses and shipwrecks, visitors can get lost in our long, lively barrier island history. In between, you can kick back, take off or glide away. There's no better place to do virtually nothing but relax or to do every conceivable activity — barring mountain climbing and downhill skiing.

There are wide-open wildlife refuges across the islands and fluorescent-lighted fish tanks at the state aquarium. You can dive into history by boarding a 16th-century representative sailing ship or scuba dive beneath the Atlantic to explore a Civil War shipwreck. Whatever your interests, you'll find outlets for them here. There's never enough time to see everything the Outer Banks has to offer.

In this chapter, we have highlighted our favorite attractions. There are many others you'll discover on your own, and locals will gladly share their own secret spots. Many of these places have free admission or request nominal donations. We begin with the northernmost communities and work southward. Each area has its own section, so pick your pleasure.

Also, be sure to read our chapters on Recreation, Watersports and Nightlife for more exciting, educational and unusual things to do on the Outer Banks.

Corolla

The Whalehead Club
Off N.C. Hwy. 12, Corolla • (252) 453-4343 ext. 35

Overlooking the windswept wetlands of Currituck Sound, this grand dame of days gone by was once the Outer Banks' biggest, most modern structure. It was built in 1925 as a hunt club for a wealthy industrialist's French wife who had been denied admission to the nearby all-male hunt clubs that dotted the barrier island marshes. The Whalehead Club remains one of the area's most charming attractions and affords a romantic trip back in time to an era of lavish accommodations, elaborate ornamentation and Gatsby-like galas that guests once enjoyed in this great house.

Currently, county officials and a dedicated group of volunteers are trying to raise funds to bring the Whalehead Club back to its former glory. The copper-roofed retreat needs restoring. The ballroom's cork floor is crumbling. The once-grand exterior is battered. Proceeds from tour fees are earmarked for restoration efforts, and officials and volunteers are also hoping to include a wildlife museum on the first floor. Recently, the 1902 Louis XIV low-signature Steinway piano that sat in the mansion for more than a half-century was sent out for repairs. For the time being, the newly revitalized instrument can be seen at the Currituck County satellite office in Corolla.

Today, visitors can still see the structure's solid mahogany doors and interior walls. The Tiffany globes from the former chandeliers, custom designed in a waterlily motif, can be seen alongside the dining room fireplace's slate hearth. The 16-room basement, which once housed an extensive wine cellar and root cellars for potatoes and onions, is no longer used for its original purpose. The bathrooms, one of the first on the Outer Banks to contain hot and cold indoor plumbing — with both salted and unsalted running water available to fill claw-foot tubs — still look inviting to vacationing house guests.

Outside, the area's first in-ground swimming pool, which once flanked the premises, has long since been demolished. The footbridge and boathouse, however, remain. You can walk the grounds of this historic hunt club for free. Tours of the mansion are offered from 10 AM to 4 PM daily from June through September. Since the Whalehead Club is staffed on a volunteer basis, hours may change according to availability of staff. There is an entry fee. Call for prices and updates.

Currituck Beach Lighthouse
Off N.C. Hwy. 12, Corolla • (252) 453-4939

The Outer Banks' northernmost lighthouse, this red-brick beacon was built in 1875 just north of the Whalehead Club in Corolla. The 214 steps to the top bring you eye to eye with the 50,000-candlepower lamp that still flashes every 20 seconds. This 158-foot-tall lighthouse is open from Palm Sunday weekend through Thanksgiving from 10 AM to 5 PM seven days a week, weather permitting. Visitors are not permitted to climb the tower during high wind conditions or lightning storms. In summer's extended daylight, the lighthouse is open until 6 PM. There is a $4 entry fee per person. The Corolla Wild Horse Fund maintains its headquarters at the base of the tower, and a museum and giftshop are also on the premises.

The Lighthouse Keepers' House, a Victorian dwelling, was constructed from pre-cut, labeled materials shipped by the U.S. Lighthouse Board on a barge and then was assembled on-site. In 1876, when the Keepers' House was completed, two keepers and their families shared the duplex in the isolated seaside setting. The house was abandoned when the lighthouse became automated and keepers were no longer needed to continually clean the lenses, trim the wicks, fuel the lamp and wind the clockwork mechanism that rotated the bright beacon.

Today, the Keepers' House is listed on the National Register of Historic Places. Outer Banks Conservationists Inc. assumed responsibility for its restoration in 1980. Exterior reconstruction already is complete, and the interior is nearly restored.

The Keepers' House is open only 12 days per year, and occasionally by special arrangement. Since the interior of the quarters is very small, public tours of the facility are not possible on a regular basis. Call for more information if you are interested in viewing the house.

Kill Devil Hills

Wright Brothers National Memorial
U.S. Hwy. 158, MP 8, Kill Devil Hills • (252) 441-7430

Set atop a steep, grassy sand hill in the center of Kill Devil Hills, the trapezoidal granite monument to Orville and Wilbur Wright is within easy walking distance of the site of the world's first powered airplane flight. Below where this lighthouse-style tower now stands, on the blustery afternoon of December 17, 1903, the two bicycle-building brothers from Dayton, Ohio, changed history by soaring over a distance of more than 852 feet and staying airborne for 59 seconds in their homemade flying machine. The monument was erected in Orville and Wilbur Wright's honor in 1932. In 1998, the circling light that sits atop the monument was restored to operation; it's sweeping flash now illuminates the night.

In the low, domed building on the right side of the main drive off U.S. 158, the National Park Service operates a visitors center, gift shop and museum. Here, people can view interpretive exhibits of man's first flight and see displays on later aviation advancements. Explanations of the Wright brothers' struggles to fly include parts of their planes, engines and notes. Reproductions of their gliders are displayed in the flight room, and rangers offer free guided historical tours year round.

Outside the exhibit center, four markers set along a sandy runway commemorate the takeoff and landing sites of each of Orville and Wilbur's December 17 flights. Reconstructed wooden sheds replicating those used at the Wrights' 1903 camp and hangar also are on the grounds and open to visitors. These sheds are furnished with tools, equipment and even cans of milk like the brothers used.

A short hike takes you from the visitors center to the monument hill, but if you'd rather drive or ride, parking is available closer to the base of the hill. Paved walkways make access easier, but cacti and sand spurs abound in the area. Also, be wary that the walk up the monument hill is longer and more strenuous than it looks, so it's best to go at a leisurely pace. On a hot summer day, consider visiting the site in the morning or late afternoon, when the sun is not as strong. This seemingly simple structure is most powerful when you can really contemplate the immensity of the brothers' accomplishment.

Besides tours, the Exhibit Center at the Wright Brothers National Memorial offers a variety of summer programs. Grounds and buildings are open to vehicles from 9 AM until 5 PM Labor Day through Memorial Day. Hours are from 9 AM to 6 PM in the summer. Thirty minute flight-room talks are given by rangers every hour on the hour year-round.

Cost for entry at the guard gate is $2 per person or $4 per car.

Photo: Courtesy of J. Aaron Trotman

There is more to the Outer Banks than just sand and waves.
Grab a canoe and explore the flora, fauna, and wildlife.

Nags Head Woods Ecological Preserve
Ocean Acres Dr., Kill Devil Hills • (252) 441-4381, (252) 441-2525

If you've had a little too much sun, or if you'd just like to spend time in a secluded forest on a part of the Outer Banks few people get to see, allocate an afternoon for the Nags Head Woods Ecological Preserve, west of U.S. Highway 158.

The Nature Conservancy, a privately funded organization dedicated to preserving pristine ecosystems, oversees this maritime forest. Although Nags Head Woods is privately owned — it is not a park — it is an example of a successful private-public partnership. A large portion of the land was donated to the nonprofit group by the Town of Nags Head. Trails are open to visitors on weekdays from 10 AM until 3 PM, while members of the Nature Conservancy are welcome anytime.

More than 4 miles of trails and tiny footbridges wind through forest, dune, swamp and pond habitats. There's an old graveyard near the site of an early 20th-century farming community that once included a school, church and dozens of homes. The maritime forest itself is well-hidden on the west side of the Outer Banks, and many rare plant and animal species abound within this virtually untouched ecosystem. See our Natural Wonders chapter for more information.

There is a small visitors center, gift shop and gazebo near the entrance. The staff offers a variety of free field trips, including guided bird walks and kayaking excursions during warm months. No camping, horseback riding, loitering, bicycling, firearms, alcoholic beverages, picnicking or pets are allowed in the preserve.

Write to the Nature Conservancy at 701 W. Ocean Acres Drive, Kill Devil Hills, NC 27948. All donations are welcome, and memberships start at $25. Monies support the preserve's environmental education and research programs.

Nags Head

Jockey's Ridge State Park
U.S. Hwy. 158, MP 12, Nags Head • (252) 441-7132

The East Coast's tallest sand dune and one of the Outer Banks most phenomenal natural attractions, Jockey's Ridge has been a favorite stop for tourists for more than 150 years. In the early 1970s, bulldozers began trying to flatten the top of the dune to make way for a housing subdivision. A Nags Head woman, Carolista Golden, single-handedly stopped the destruction and formed a committee that saved Jockey's Ridge.

State officials made the sand hill a protected park in 1975, but the dunes are unruly subjects. The sand mountains have migrated southwest in fits and starts over the decades. In the past 25 years, the steepest side of the hill has shifted more than 1,500 feet to the southwest. Jockey's Ridge is also getting shorter. At the turn of the century, the highest mound was estimated at 140 feet tall. In 1971, it was about 110 feet tall. Development has blocked replenishment of the sand, and nearby grasses have caught the blowing sand before it reaches the ridge.

Today, the 1.5-mile-long, 420-acre-plus dune — which varies from 90 feet to 110 feet in height — is open to the public year round until sunset. It's a popular spot for hang gliders, summer hikers, small children who like to roll down the steep slopes and teenagers who delight in flinging and flipping themselves dramatically down the sandy hills. In 1997, more than 940,000 people visit Jockey's Ridge, making it one of North Carolina's most popular parks.

Getting to Jockey's Ridge has been easier since state Department of Transportation workers installed a crosswalk across U.S. 158 a few summers ago. If you park at Kitty Hawk Connection, where the colorful flags are flying on the east side of the highway, you can walk across the road and enter the state park on foot. If you'd rather drive in, park headquarters is near the northern end of a parking lot off the west side of U.S. 158. You'll notice an entrance sign at MP 12, Carolista Drive in Nags Head.

A new visitor's center, a museum and a giftshop were recently completed near park headquarters. Centered around the theme of wind and how it affects Jockey's Ridge, the free museum features photo displays of the history and recreation at the dune and a diorama of the animals that inhabit the area. Information panels of plants and animals and an auditorium where slide shows and videos are shown is also at the facility. Maps available from the park ranger indicate walking areas. Two trails — the new Soundside Nature Trail, a very easy 45-minute walk, and Tracks in the Sand, a moderate 1.5-mile trek — are on-site for hikers looking for a change of scenery. Jockey's Ridge State Park offers natural history programs throughout the summer, including stargazing and wildlife discovery evening hikes and early-morning bird-watching and natural history discovery adventures. Programs for kids are also offered, but rangers warn that they fill up early and many require advance registration. Sheltered picnic areas also are available for leisurely lunches. Call for program schedules.

It's a long, hot hike to the top of the ridge, but it's well worth the work. Bring shoes or boots. Don't try it barefoot; you'll burn your feet. Also, some lower areas around the dune are covered with broken glass. From the top of Jockey's Ridge, you can see both ocean and sound. Cottages along the beach look like tiny huts from a miniature train set. Kite-flying and hang-gliding enthusiasts catch the breezes that flow constantly around the steep summit, shifting the sand in all directions. The desert-like appearance of the sand dunes reveals strange but artistic patterns of winds and of footprints made by people climbing the hills.

If your mobility is impaired, there's a 360-foot boardwalk that affords wheelchairs and baby strollers a slightly sloping incline onto a wooden platform overlooking the center of the dune. For the visually handicapped, audio guides are available at the park office. Park rangers can also provide a ride to the top of the dune if you call in advance.

Roanoke Island

The Elizabethan Gardens
Off U.S. Hwy. 64, Roanoke Island • (252) 473-3234

Created by the Garden Club of North Carolina Inc. in 1960 to commemorate the efforts of Raleigh's colonists at establishing an English settlement, these magnificent botanical gardens offer an exquisite, aromatic environment year round. They include 10½ acres of the state's most colorful, dazzling flora. The flower-filled walkways are the perfect contrast to the windblown, barren Outer Banks beaches.

Six full-time gardeners tend more than 1,000 varieties of immaculately manicured trees, shrubs and flowers in the Elizabethan Gardens, which you'll find north of Manteo. Translucent emerald grass fringes marble fountains, and beauty blooms from every crevice.

Visitors enter at the Great Gate into formal gardens along curving walkways carefully crafted from brick and sand. The bricks were handmade at the Silas Lucas Kiln, in operation during the late 1800s in Wilson, North Carolina. The tree-lined landscape is divided into a dozen gardens.

Although this botanical refuge is breathtakingly beautiful all year, offering different colors and fragrances depending on the season, it is, perhaps, the most striking in spring. Azaleas, dogwood, pansies, wisteria and tulips bloom around every bend. Rhododendron, roses, lacecap and other hydrangea appear in May. Summer brings fragrant gardenias, colorful annuals and perennials, magnolia, crape myrtle, Oriental lilies and herbs. Chrysanthemums and the changing colors of leaves signal the beginning of autumn and camellias bloom from late fall through winter.

In the center of the paths, six marble steps down from the rest of the greenery, the crowned jewel of the Elizabethan Gardens awaits discovery. A sunken garden, complete with Roman statuary, tiered fountains and low shrubs pruned into geometric flower frames springs from the sandy soil. The famous Virginia Dare statue nearby is based on an Indian legend that says Virginia, the first English child born in America, grew up among Native Americans (see our Roanoke Island chapter).

The Elizabethan Gardens are open daily from 9 AM to 5 PM except Saturday and Sunday in December, January and February. Shoulder season hours are adjusted according to available daylight. The gardens are closed Christmas and New Year's Day. From June 1 through September 1, the gardens will stay open until 7 PM. Admission is $3 for adults, $1 for youths ages 12 through 17 and free for children younger than 12. There is no fee in the winter. Season passes are offered for $7.

Wheelchairs are provided. Most paths are handicapped-accessible. Some plants are for sale in the garden gift shop. The gardens also are a favorite wedding locale, and a meeting room is available for a fee to community groups up to 100 people.

Fort Raleigh National Historic Site
Off U.S. Hwy. 64, Roanoke Island • (252) 473-5772

Don't visit Fort Raleigh and expect to see a fort. What exists on the site is a small earthworks fortification. It's no daunting barricade, but is a lovely spot drenched in American history. On the north end of Roanoke Island, near the Roanoke Sound's shores, Fort Raleigh marks the beginning of English settlement in North America.

Designated as a National Historic Site in 1941, this more than 500-acre expanse of woods and beach includes the "outerwork" — an area built intentionally away from living space — where 1585 colonist Joachim Gans smote copper, along with the National Park Service's Cape Hatteras National Seashore visitors center and headquarters, and a nature trail. An outdoor exhibit about the Freedman's colony, a community the government established for escaped slaves between 1862 and 1867, is also on-site. Fort Raleigh incorporates Weirs Point and Fort Huger, significant historic markers to radio and war, respectively.

At the Roanoke Island base of the bridge to Manns Harbor, Weirs Point is an attractive public beach on the Croatan Sound. Free parking is available at the turnoff on Roanoke Island just before the end of the bridge. The brackish water is warm and shallow and perfect for kids. The beach is also wide enough to allow for a good game of Frisbee or a pleasant family picnic. About 300 yards north of Weirs Point, in 6 feet of water, lay the remains of Fort Huger. This was the largest Confederate fort on the island when Union troops advanced across the Outer Banks during the Civil War battles of 1862. The island has migrated quite a bit in the last 130 years. The fort used to sit securely on the north end on solid land.

In 1901, from a hut on Weirs Point beach, one of the unsung geniuses of the electrical age began investigating what was then called "wireless telegraphy." Reginald Fessenden held hundreds of patents on radiotelephony and electronics but died without credit for many of them. In a letter dated "April 3, 1902, Manteo," Fessenden tells his patent attorney that "I can now telephone as far as I can telegraph. . . . I have sent varying musical notes from Hatteras and received them here with but 3 watts of energy." The world's first musical radio broadcasts were completed on this soundside sand of the Outer Banks.

Picnic benches, a Dare County information kiosk and restrooms are provided at Weirs Point. Watch for stumps and broken stakes in the water. The tide also creeps up quickly, so beware of needing to move beach blankets away from its encroaching flow.

The Fort Raleigh visitors center offers interpretive exhibits in its small museum. A 17-minute video provides an introduction to this historic site. Here, the 400-year-old Elizabethan Room from Heronden Hall in Kent, England, is on display. William Randolph Hearst had the room transported to the United States after he had it removed from an authentic 16th-century house. The furnishings, carved man-

It's not unusual to see dolphins frolicking in these Atlantic waters.

telpiece, paneling, stone fireplace and blown glass in the leaded windows offer a glimpse of America's origins across the ocean.

Self-guided tours and tours led by Park Service personnel are available at this archaeologically significant site. Programs vary depending on the time of day and year. The Thomas Hariot Nature Trail is a short, self-guided trail with pine-needle paths that lead to the sandy shores of Roanoke Sound. Some believe that Sir Richard Grenville first stepped ashore here on Roanoke Island in the late 16th century.

Interpretive programs on African-American history, European colonial history, Native American history and Civil War history are offered in the summer. Fort Raleigh National Historic Site is open year round from 9 AM until 5 PM seven days a week. Hours are extended in the summer. Fort Raleigh is closed Christmas Day.

The Lost Colony
Off U.S. Hwy. 64, Waterside Theatre, Roanoke Island
• (252) 473-3414, (800) 488-5012

The nation's longest running outdoor drama, this historical account of the first English settlement in North America is a must-see for Outer Banks visitors. Pulitzer Prize-winning author Paul Green brought the history of English colonization to life through an impressive combination of Elizabethan music, Native American dances, colorful costumes and vivid drama on a soundside stage in 1937. His play continues to enchant audiences today at Waterside Theatre, near Fort Raleigh, on Roanoke Island.

After record-breaking attendance in 1997, the 60th anniversary of *The Lost Colony* production, the 1998 season also promises to be exciting. Not only will the audience have use of bigger bathrooms and concession areas, but they will, for the first time, sit in brand-new stadium seats, rather than the rough-hewn benches in place for decades. In essence, it will be almost a totally new amphitheater. The pre-show production both leading to and inside the theater that was revamped considerably last year by Tony-award-winning Broadway designer William Ivey Long will again be part of the show. Spectacular new scenery and costume designs will be featured changes in the 61st season.

The Lost Colony is a theatrical account of Sir Walter Raleigh's early explorers who first settled on the shores near the present day theater in 1585. (Andy Griffith got his start playing Sir Walter Raleigh for several seasons). Children and adults are equally captivated by the performers, staging and music; many locals see the show every year and always find it spellbinding. If you have youngsters, come early and have them sit in the very front row by the stage. They'll never stop talking about it! It can get chilly on evenings when the wind blows off the sound, so we recommend sweaters, even in July and August. Mosquitoes at this outdoor drama also can be vicious, especially after a rain, so bring plenty of bug repellent. The theater is wheelchair-accessible and the staff is glad to accommodate special customers.

Once you arrive, settle back and enjoy a thoroughly professional, well-rehearsed, technically outstanding show. The leads are played by professional actors. Most of the backstage personnel are pros too — and it shows. Supporting actors are often locals, with some island residents passing from part to part as they grow up. On August 18, a local infant is chosen to reenact Virginia Dare's birthday.

All shows start at 8:30 PM and are performed nightly except Saturday. The season opens June 5 and runs through August 28. Tickets are $14 for adults, $7 for children 12 and younger and $13 for senior citizens. Adult-accompanied children 12 and younger are admitted at half price for Sunday and Monday night performances. Those 65 and older are admitted for $12 on Fridays. North Carolina residents will be admitted for half-price on Fridays and Sundays in June. Groups of 20 or more can call for a discount.

This is probably the most popular summertime event on the Outer Banks, and we recommend you make reservations, though you can try your luck at the door if you wish. You can make paid mail reservations by writing The Lost Colony, 1409 Highway 64/264, Manteo, North Carolina 27954; or you can reserve tickets by phone. Tickets can also be purchased at 70 outlets across the Outer Banks. Call for locations. Unpaid reservations will be held at the box office for pickup until 7:30 PM. If a production is rained out, ticket holders can come back any other night any other week, month or year.

North Carolina Aquarium
Airport Rd., Roanoke Island • (252) 473-3493

Down a winding road northwest of Manteo near the Dare County airport, the North Carolina Aquarium at Roanoke Island offers an air-conditioned, indoor excursion that's open all year.

Accessibly set up and labeled to provide a detailed glimpse of sea life along North Carolina's barrier islands, this educational attraction includes an 8,400-gallon, wall-size, well-lighted shark tank; a video of on-site osprey nesting near the parking lot; state laboratories and a marine reference library; and a touch-me tank where visitors can pet horseshoe crabs and watch saltwater fish scurrying through shallow ponds.

Fluorescent lights glow like jewels along long, darkened corridors where sea turtles float on iridescent driftwood, long-nose gar bump against the glass walls of their world, and octopi and burrfish dive through their tanks, swirling sand. Sea life starts out with freshwater species at the aquarium, shading through brackish to saltwater. A wetlands exhibit features freshwater turtles and amphibians, including some small alligators. Be aware that because the aquarium is in the process of expansion, some exhibits may not always be available to view. Call ahead for updates.

Visitors can view films on marine and biological topics. Staff members conduct summer daytime field trips and talks for all age groups. Check at the front desk for a monthly calendar of events, or consult *The Coast* free weekly newspaper. The aquarium caters to groups of any kind and can supply meeting facilities in its conference room, seminar room or 240-seat auditorium. There's also a great gift shop with marine-related collectibles, books and T-shirts.

To reach the aquarium, drive north from Manteo on U.S. 64. Turn left on Airport Road, following signs to the airport. After the big 90-degree turn in the road, the aquarium will be on the right. It's open year-round from 9 AM to 5 PM every day except Thanksgiving, Christmas and New Year's Day. Admission is $3 for adults, $2 for senior citizens and active military, $1 for children ages 6 to 17 and free for children younger than 6. Aquarium Society members are admitted free.

Roanoke Island Festival Park and the Elizabeth II
One Festival Park, Manteo • (252) 475-1500, (252) 475-1506 24-hour events line

An expansion of the Elizabeth II Historic Site, Roanoke Island Festival Park is the newest — and most ambitious — attraction on the Outer Banks. Funded by a $10 million state appropriation, the new history, education and cultural arts project will include an 8,500-square-foot hall of interactive exhibits; a film theater featuring *The Legend of Two-Path*, a 45-minute film depicting the first landing of English settlers from the Native American perspective; an outdoor performance pavilion with lawn seating for 3,500 people; an art gallery and public meeting space; a museum shop; and the *Elizabeth II* sailing vessel.

Visitors can explore the evolution of Roanoke Island and the Outer Banks from the late 16th century though the early 1900s through living history interpretation, exhibits, film, and visual and performing arts programs.

The *Elizabeth II*, designed as the centerpiece for the 400th anniversary of the first English settlement in America, is a representative sailing ship similar to the one that carried Sir Walter Raleigh's colonists across the Atlantic in 1585. Interpreters clad in Elizabethan costumes conduct tours of the colorful, 69-foot ship.

Although it was built in 1983, the *Elizabeth II*'s story really began four centuries earlier, when Thomas Cavendish mortgaged his estates to build the *Elizabeth II* for England's second expedition to Roanoke Island. With six other vessels, the original *Elizabeth* made the first colonization voyage to the New World 1585 and landed on the Outer Banks.

There wasn't enough information available about the original vessels to reconstruct one, so shipbuilders used the designs of vessels from 1585 to build the state boat. Constructed entirely in a wooden structure on the Manteo waterfront, the completed ship, *Elizabeth II*, slid down hand-greased rails into Shallowbag Bay in front of a crowd of enthusiastic dignitaries and locals in 1983.

Stretching 69 feet long, 17 feet wide and drawing 8 feet of water, the *Elizabeth II* cost $750,000 to build and was funded entirely through private donations. Its decks are hand-hewn from juniper timbers. Its frames, keel, planking and decks are fastened with 7,000 locust wood pegs.

Every baulk, spar, block and lift of the state ship are as close to authentic as possible, with only three exceptions: a wider upper-deck hatch for easier visitor access; a vertical hatch in the afterdeck to make steering easier for the helmsman; and a controversial pair of diesel engines that were installed in the *Elizabeth II* in 1993. The 115-horsepower motors help the grand sailing ship move under its own power, instead of relying on expensive tug boats that had to tow it before. Now, the vessel can cruise up to 8 knots per hour with no wind and travel for up to 40 hours without refilling its two 150-gallon gas tanks. The state ship stays on the Outer Banks most of the year, but during the off-seasons, it sometimes travels to other North Carolina ports, acting as an emissary for its Roanoke Island home and serving as the state's only moving historic site. Roanoke Island Festival Park is open year round. Hours vary according to season. Admission is $8 for adults, $4 for students and free for children under 5. Group rates are available.

Bodie Island

Bodie Island Lighthouse and Keepers' Quarters
West of N.C. Hwy. 12, Bodie Island • (252) 441-5711

This black-and-white beacon with horizontal bands is one of four lighthouses still standing along the Outer Banks. It sits more than a half-mile from the sea, in a field of green grass. The site, 6 miles south of Whalebone Junction, is a perfect place to picnic.

In 1870, the federal government bought 15 acres of land for $150 on which to build the lighthouse and keepers quarters. When the project was finished two years later, Bodie Island Lighthouse was very close to the inlet and stood 150 feet tall and was the only lighthouse between Cape Henry, Virginia, and Cape Hatteras. The inlet is now migrating away from the beacon, which is the third to stand near Oregon Inlet since the inlet opened during an 1846 hurricane. The first light developed cracks and had to be removed. Confederate soldiers destroyed the second tower to frustrate Union shipping efforts.

Wanchese resident Vernon Gaskill served as the last civilian lightkeeper of Bodie Island Lighthouse. As late as 1940, he said, the tower was the only structure between Oregon Inlet and Jockey's Ridge. Gaskill helped his father strain kerosene before pouring it into the light. The kerosene prevented particles from clogging the vaporizer that kept the beacon burning.

Today, the lighthouse grounds and keeper's quarters offer a welcome respite during the drive to Hatteras Island. Wide expanses of marshland behind the tower offer enjoyable walks through cattails, yaupon and wax myrtle. A boardwalk will keep your feet dry.

The National Park Service added new exhibits to the Bodie Island keepers quarters in 1995. The visitors center there is open daily from mid-March through December. Hours are 9 AM to 6 PM, except after Labor Day when the facility closes at 5 PM. The lighthouse itself is not open, but you can look up the tall tower from below when volunteers are present to open the structure. Even a quick drive around the grounds to see the exterior is worth it.

Coquina Beach
N.C. Hwy. 12, Bodie Island

Once one of the widest beaches on the Outer Banks, Coquina Beach, 6 miles south of Whalebone Junction, was heavily damaged during 1993 and 1994 storms. The National Park Service expanded and repaved parking areas, and in 1996 it opened a spanking new bathhouse, restrooms and outdoor shower facilities.

This remote area, miles away from any business or rental cottage, is still a superb spot to fish, surf, swim or sunbathe. The sand is almost white and the beach and offshore areas are relatively flat.

Drawing its name from the tiny butterfly-shaped coquina clams that burrow into the beach, at times almost every inch of this portion of the federally protected Cape Hatteras National Seashore harbors hundreds of recently washed up shells and several species of rare shorebirds. Coquinas are edible and can be collected and cleaned from their shells to make a fishy-tasting chowder. Local brick makers also have used them as temper in buildings.

Oregon Inlet Fishing Center
N.C. 12, Bodie Island • (252) 441-6301, (800) 272-5199

Sportfishing enthusiasts, or anyone remotely interested in offshore angling, must stop by this bustling charter boat harbor on the north shore of Oregon Inlet. Set beside the U.S. Coast Guard station on land controlled by the National Park Service, Oregon Inlet Fishing Center is a federal concessionaire, so all vessels charge the same rate. A day on the Atlantic with one of these captains may give rise to a marlin, sailfish, wahoo, tuna or dolphin on the end of the line. See our Fishing chapter for details.

Hatteras Island

Pea Island National Wildlife Refuge
Northern Hatteras Island, N.C. Hwy. 12 • (252) 987-2394

Pea Island National Wildlife Refuge begins at the southern base of the Herbert C. Bonner Bridge and is the first place you'll come to if you enter Hatteras Island from the north. The beach along this undeveloped stretch of sand is popular with anglers, surfers, sunbathers and shell seekers. On the right side of the road, heading south, salt marshes surround Pamlico Sound, and birds seem to flutter from every grove of cattails.

Founded on April 12, 1938, Pea Island refuge was federally funded as a winter preserve for snow geese. President Roosevelt put his Civilian Conservation Corps to work stabilizing the slightly sloping dunes, building them up with bulldozers, erecting long expanses of sand fencing and securing the sand with sea oats and grasses. Workers built dikes near the sound to form ponds and freshwater marshes. They planted fields to provide food for the waterfowl.

With 5,915 acres that attract nearly 400 observed species of birds, Pea Island is an outdoor aviary well worth venturing off the road, and into the wilderness, to visit. Few tourists visited this refuge when Hatteras Island was cut off from the rest of the Outer Banks, and people arrived at the southern beaches by ferry. After the Oregon Inlet bridge opened in 1964, motorists began driving through this once isolated outpost.

Today, Pea Island is one of the barrier islands' most popular havens for bird watchers, naturalists and sea-turtle savers. Endangered species from the loggerhead sea turtle to the tiny piping plover shorebirds inhabit this enchanted area. Pea Island's name comes from the "dune peas" that grow all along the now grassy sand dunes. The tiny plant with pink and lavender flowers is a favorite food of migrating geese.

If you enter the refuge from the north on N.C. 12, note the new roadbed that was completed in December 1995. This 3-mile stretch of highway had to be moved more than 300 feet west of its former site to get it farther away from the waves. During 1994, state officials had to shut down the two-lane road at least three times because the ocean had washed across it, spilling up to 2 feet of sand in some spots.

To keep the road clear and provide a more permanent pathway through the Outer Banks, transportation engineers decided to reroute the most threatened portion of the pavement closer to the sound. The project cost taxpayers about $3 million. Since 1990, state transportation officials have spent more than $31 million trying to keep N.C. 12 open. They invested another $18 million in routine maintenance on the road. Special efforts have included a $1.8 million beach nourishment project to pump sand back on the beach and $920,000 worth of sandbags stacked along the shore. Against the objections of Dare County officials, the sandbags were removed during the summer of 1996 because state officials deemed them a temporary measure that would be harmful to the shoreline if they remained in place any longer.

Four miles south of the Bonner Bridge's southern base, at the entrance to the new portion of N.C. 12, the Pea Island Visitor Center offers free parking and easy access to the beach. If you walk directly across the highway to the top of the dunes, you'll see the remains of the more than century-old federal transport *Oriental*. Her steel boiler is the black mass, all that remains since the ship sank in May 1862.

On the sound side of the highway, in the marshes, ponds and endless wetlands, whistling swans, snow geese, Canada geese and 25 species of ducks make winter sojourns through the refuge.

Savannah sparrows, migrant warblers, gulls, terns, herons and egrets also alight in this area from fall through early spring. In summer, American avocets, willets, black-necked stilts and several species of ducks nest here.

Bug repellent is a must on Pea Island from March through October. Besides insects, ticks may also cause problems. Check your clothing before getting back in the car, and shower as soon as possible if you hike through any underbrush.

Chicamacomico Life Saving Station
N.C. Hwy. 12, Rodanthe • (252) 987-1552

With volunteer labor and long years of dedication, this once decrepit lifesaving station is now beautifully restored and open for tours. Its weathered, silvery-shingled buildings sparkle on the sandy lawn, which is surrounded by a perfect picket fence. Even the out-buildings have been brought back to their former uses.

Chicamacomico was one of the Outer Banks' original seven lifesaving stations, opening in 1874 at its current site. The present boathouse building was the original station but was retained as a storage shed when the bigger facility was built. Under three keepers with the last name of Midgett, Chicamacomico crews guarded the sea along Hatteras Island's northern coast for 70 years. Between 1876 and the time the station closed in 1954, seven Midgetts were awarded the Gold Life Saving Award; three won the silver, and six others worked or lived at Chicamacomico. Perhaps the station's most famous rescue was when surfmen pulled crew members from the British tanker *Mirlo* off their burning ship and into safety.

Today the nonprofit Chicamacomico Historical Association oversees and operates the lifesaving station. Volunteers set up a museum of area lifesaving awards and artifacts in the main building and have recovered some of the lifesaving equipment for the boathouse. Volunteers take school groups on tours of the station, showing them how the breeches buoy helped rescue shipwreck victims and explaining the precise maneuvers surfmen had to follow on shore.

Costumed re-enactments of beach apparatus drills are held every Thursday in summer from 2 through 5 PM. The building is open from 11 AM to 5 PM Tuesday, Thursday and Saturday in-season. Hours may be extended if volunteers are available. The interior restoration was completed in 1998, and new photo, video and lifesaving service artifacts are on display. To help support the lifesaving station and the Chicamacomico Historical Association, send donations to the association at P.O. Box 140, Rodanthe, NC 27968.

Cape Hatteras National Seashore

Hatteras Island Visitors Center, off N.C. Hwy. 12, Buxton • (252) 995-4474

About 300 yards south of Old Lighthouse Road, a large wooden sign welcomes visitors to the Cape Hatteras National Seashore and Hatteras Island Visitors Center. Turn left if you're heading south, toward the split-rail fence, and follow the winding road past turtle ponds and marshes.

If you turn left at the fork in this road, you'll head toward the Cape Hatteras Lighthouse and the National Park Service Visitors Center. Turn right, and you'll wind up at the Cape Point campground. Surf fishing, sunbathing, swimming, surfing and four-wheel driving are allowed along most areas of the beach here year round.

The visitors center is near the lighthouse, past a newly expanded parking area. It's in the former house of the assistant lighthouse keepers, which was built in 1854. This two-story, wooden frame home was renovated in 1986 and is adjacent to the smaller keepers' quarters. It houses an extensive museum of lifesaving artifacts and lighthouse memorabilia. Free exhibits include information on shipping, wars and Outer Banks heroes.

A small bookstore in the visitors center sells literature on lifesaving stations, lighthouses and Hatteras Island history. Clean restrooms also are available here. Volunteers offer a range of summer interpretive programs on the visitor center's wide, covered front porch. Activities change seasonally, with fall and spring programs also conducted. Call ahead for a schedule, or pick one up at the information desk inside.

The visitors center is open from 9 AM to 5 PM daily from September through mid-June and from 9 AM to 6 PM from mid-June through Labor Day. It's closed Christmas Day.

Cape Hatteras Lighthouse

Off N.C. Hwy. 12, Buxton • (252) 995-4474

The nation's tallest brick lighthouse, this black and white striped beacon is open for free tours throughout the summer and is well worth the climb for hearty hikers. It contains 268 spiraling stairs — 257 which are open to the public — and an 800,000-candlepower electric light that rotates every 7.5 seconds. Its bright beacon can be seen about 20 miles out to sea.

The original Cape Hatteras Lighthouse was built in 1803 to guard the "Graveyard of the Atlantic." The tower sat by its present location near Cape Point. Just off this eastern edge of the Outer Banks, the warm Gulf Stream meets the cold Labrador Current, creating dangerous undercurrents around the ever-shifting offshore shoals.

Standing 90 feet tall and sitting about 300 yards south of its current site, the first lighthouse at Cape Hatteras was fueled with whale oil, which didn't burn bright enough to illuminate the dark shoals surrounding it. Erosion weakened the structure over the years, and in 1861, retreating Confederate soldiers took the light's lens with them, leaving Hatteras Island in the dark.

The lighthouse that's still standing was erected in 1870 on a floating foundation and cost $150,000 to build. More than 1.25 million Philadelphia baked bricks are included in the 180-foot tall tower. A special Fresnel lens that refracts the light increases its visibility.

Although the lighthouse is still holding its ground, the beach around its octagonal base is eroding rapidly. Workers stacked sandbags around the structure and have added three rock groins in the ocean nearby to stop sand movement. The National Park Service plans to move the lighthouse 1,500 feet inland if the federal government funds the estimated $12 million project

Staffed entirely by volunteers, the Cape Hatteras Lighthouse is open all the way to the outdoor tower at the top. The breathtaking view is like looking off the roof of a 20-story building, and the free adventure is well worth the effort. The climb is strenuous, so don't attempt to carry children in your arms or in kid carriers. Climbing is permitted starting at 9:30 AM from Easter weekend through Columbus Day. In the summer, the tower is open until 4 PM. In the shoulder seasons, the lighthouse closes at 2 PM. Hours are subject to change, so call first. Climbing is always subject to weather conditions.

Ocracoke Island

Ocracoke Pony Pens
N.C. Hwy. 12, Ocracoke Island

According to local legends, ships carrying the first English colonists to America made their initial landing at Ocracoke Inlet in 1585. The flagship *Tiger* grounded on a shallow shoal. Sir Richard Grenville ordered the vessel, including a load of horses purchased in the West Indies, unloaded so the ship would float again. Some of the sturdy beasts, it is said, swam ashore to run wild on Ocracoke.

Other theories say the ponies were refugees from Spanish ship-wrecks. A few practical people insist they were merely brought to Ocracoke by early inhabitants and allowed to roam freely because — on an island miles from anything else in the Atlantic — there is really no reason to fence in a herd of horses. In any case, Ocracoke's "wild" horses have survived on this Outer Banks island for at least two centuries. In the late 1900s, old-timers said, hundreds ran around eating marsh grass and splashing in the shallow salt marshes.

As populations grew, however, some of the animals were auctioned off. Boy Scout troops used to round up the wild horses annually. When the National Park Service began overseeing the federal seashore, they began managing the wild herd. Today, about two dozen ponies live in a large penned area off N.C. 12, about 6 miles southwest of the Hatteras-Ocracoke ferry dock. There's a small parking area off the road and a raised, wooden observation platform overlooking the mile-long fenced pasture. Sometimes the horses come right up near the road, posing for pictures. Other times, especially in bad weather, they huddle in shelters closer to the sound and can't be seen.

Don't climb into the horse pen or attempt to feed or pet the ponies. These are wild animals that can kick and bite.

Ocracoke Island Visitors Center
N.C. Hwy. 12, Ocracoke Village • (252) 928-4531

This seasonal visitors center at the southern end of N.C. 12 is a clearinghouse of information about Ocracoke Island. It's run by the National Park Service across from Silver Lake. If you're arriving on the island from the Hatteras ferry, stay on the main road, turn right at the lake and continue around it, counterclockwise, until you see the low brown building on your right. Free parking is available at the visitors center.

Inside, there's an information desk, helpful staff, a small book shop and exhibits about Ocracoke. You can arrange to use the Park Service's docks here, and pick up maps of the winding back roads that make great bicycle paths.

The visitors center is open March through December from 9 AM to 5 PM. Hours are extended in the summer. Rangers offer a variety of free summer programs through the center, including beach and sound hikes, pirate plays, bird-watching, night hikes and history lectures. Check at the front desk for changing weekly schedules. Restrooms are open to the public in season.

Ocracoke Island Museum and Preservation Society
Silver Lake, Ocracoke Village • (252) 928-7375

By the Cedar Island ferry docks built by David Williams, the first chief of the Ocracoke Coast Guard Station, this two-story, white-frame house was moved to its present location on National Park Service land in 1989. It's east of the Park Service parking lot, on the same side of Silver Lake as the Coast Guard Station. It was recently restored and is now managed by the Ocracoke Preservation Society as a museum and visitors center. A visit to this museum provides a wonderful peek into Ocracoke as it once was, with old furnishings donated by local families and original photographs of natives filling every room. The kitchen even has its table set in authentic old silverware and dishes. Upstairs, the museum has a small research library that the public can use with museum personnel's permission. This free museum is open daily from 9 AM to 6 PM from April 1 through November.

Ocracoke Inlet Lighthouse
Southwest corner of Ocracoke Village

The southernmost of the Outer Banks' four lighthouses, this whitewashed tower also is the oldest and shortest. It stands 75 feet tall, a good walk away from any water and has an iron-railed tower set askew on the top. The lighthouse isn't open for tours or climbing, but volunteers occasionally staff its broad base, offering historical talks and answering visitors' questions. Inquire about possible staffing times at the visitors center or National Park Service offices.

Ocracoke's lighthouse is still operating, emitting one long flash every few seconds from a half-hour before sunset to a half-hour after sunrise. It was built in 1823 to replace Shell Castle Rock lighthouse, which was set offshore closer to the dangerous shoals in Ocracoke Inlet. Shell Castle light was abandoned in 1798 when the inlet shifted south.

The beam from Ocracoke's beacon rotates 360 degrees and can be seen 14 miles out to sea. The tower itself is brick, covered by hand-spread, textured white mortar. The walls are 5 feet thick at the base.

On the right side of the wooden boardwalk leading to the lighthouse, a two-story, white cottage once served as quarters for the tower's keeper. The National Park Service renovated this structure in the 1980s. It now serves as the home of Ocracoke's ranger and the structure's maintenance supervisor.

To reach the light, turn left off N.C. 12 at the Island Inn and go about 800 yards down the two-lane street. You can park near a white picketed turnoff on the right. Visitors must walk the last few yards down the boardwalk to the lighthouse.

British Cemetery
British Cemetery Rd., Ocracoke Village

Beneath a stead of trees, on the edge of a community cemetery, four granite gravestones commemorate the crew of the British vessel HMS *Bedfordshire*. This 170-foot trawler was one of a fleet of 24 antisubmarine ships that Prime Minister Winston Churchill loaned the United States in April 1942 to stave off German U-boats. On May 11 of that year, a German submarine torpedoed and sank the British ship about 40 miles south of Ocracoke.

All four officers and 33 enlisted men aboard the *Bedfordshire* drowned. U.S. Coast Guard officers stationed on Ocracoke found four of the bodies washed ashore three days later. They were able to identify two of the sailors. Townspeople gave Britain a 12-by-14-foot plot of land and buried the seamen in a site adjacent to the island's cemetery.

Since then, Coast Guard officers have maintained the grassy area within a white picket fence. They fly a British flag above the graves, and each year, on the anniversary of the sailors' deaths, the local military establishment sponsors a ceremony to honor the men who died so far from their own shores.

Portsmouth Island
South of Ocracoke Island, by private boat access

The only ghost town on the Eastern Seaboard, Portsmouth Village is about a 20-minute boat ride south of Ocracoke Island and was once the biggest town on the Outer Banks. Today, the 23-mile-long, 1.5-mile-wide island is owned and managed by The National Park Service as part of Cape Lookout National Seashore. Wilderness camping, hiking, fishing and other activities are available on the wide beach. Free, self-guided walking tours of the village are an outstanding way to see how islanders lived in the 19th century.

Capt. Rudy Austin runs daily round-trip boat shuttles throughout the summer from Silver Lake on Ocracoke Island across the Pamlico Sound to Portsmouth Island. His boat leaves at 9:30 AM from the docks and picks up passengers on Portsmouth at 2 PM. Cost is $15 per person for groups of six or more people. For groups of less than six, the charge is $20 per person. Kids up to age 12 are half-price. The scheduled trip to Portsmouth Island is available from June through September, and is available at flexible times in the off-season. Other trips in the surrounding area can also be arranged. Call at least one day ahead for reservations, (252) 928-4361 or (252) 928-5431.

Recreation

The Outer Banks is a resort area offering many amusements that families can enjoy together, such as biking, mini-golfing and dolphin tours. There are also plenty of activities to challenge the mild-mannered and chill the daredevils, with hang gliding, Jet Skiing and parasailing. Some activities are unique to these wind-swept barrier beaches; others are just ways to spend time relaxing or having fun under the sun on these beautiful islands.

You can spend an afternoon walking the wide beaches searching for shells and pieces of bright cobalt beach glass that have been polished smooth by the sand and seasons of waves. Buy the kids a kite and help them send it soaring atop the wafting winds. Bird-watching opportunities abound in the wildlife refuges north of Duck and south of Pea Island. Nags Head Woods offers both a shady respite during the heat of summer and a great place to take se-cluded hikes through one of the most marvelous preserved mari-time forests on the Atlantic seaboard. Horseshoes and pickup vol-leyball games are scattered along many public beach accesses for those who prefer working up a sweat and finding a little friendly competition. Bike paths line roads along the sounds and the sea, through towns and even along the Wright Brothers National Monu-ment. If you just need to get to sea for a while and enjoy the Outer Banks from a different vantage point, riding the state ferry to Ocra-coke Island is one of our favorite year-round pastimes. Best of all, each of those activities is free!

If bingo is your bag, several fire stations and civic clubs along the barrier islands host regularly scheduled sessions in the early eve-nings throughout the summer. Colington Island's Volunteer Fire Department off Colington Road, 441-6234, and Nags Head's Fire Department on U.S. Highway 158 just south of the Outer Banks Mall, 441-5909, are home to two of the area's more popular part-time bingo parlors.

For home entertainment, video rental stores also are scattered from Corolla to Ocracoke. Most stores don't require memberships, and they almost all rent videocassette recorders you can take back to your hotel room or vacation cottage for a night or a week.

Even Insiders who have lived here for years have not yet experienced all the recreational opportunities the Outer Banks has to offer. We sure have fun trying though.

Airplane Tours

The best way to get a feel for how fragile these barrier islands are is to take a plane ride above the Outer Banks. Small planes offer tours daily most of the year from Corolla through Ocracoke. Pilots are always pleased to dip their passengers over a school of dolphins frolicking in the Atlantic, circle one of the four lighthouses beaming from these beaches or cruise around the Wright Brothers National Monument where Wilbur and Orville flew the world's first successful heavier-than-air flights. Bring your camera. These treetop adventures provide great photo opportunities of both sea and sound shores of the islands and a true glimpse at these waterlogged wetlands. Trips can be catered to fit any desire and are well worth the reasonable rates to obtain a bird's-eye view of these skinny ribbons of sand.

Reservations are strongly recommended at least a day in advance of takeoff. All flights depend on the wind and the weather. Charter flights to Norfolk and other areas of the Outer Banks also are offered through most of these companies. Several services offer flight instruction to obtain a pilot's license and certification.

Kitty Hawk Aero Tours
Wright Brothers Airstrip, Kill Devil Hills • (252) 441-4460

OBX Air Tours
408 Airport Rd., Roanoke Island • (252) 473-3222, (252) 453-9337, (888) 289-8202

Island Flying Service
Frisco Shopping Center, N.C. Hwy. 12, Frisco • (252) 995-6671

Pelican Airways
Ocracoke Airstrip, Ocracoke • (252) 928-1661

All-Terrain Vehicles

One of the most exhilarating ways to see the off-road areas of the

Outer Banks is on an all-terrain vehicle. Whether you're cruising along the beach or chasing a sunset up the marshy sounds, you get closer to nature on one of these low-to-the-ground, open-air, gasoline-powered dune buggies. But keep in mind you're limited to 15 mph, and you can't play on the dunes.

Corolla Outback Adventures
Wee Winks Shopping Center, N.C. Hwy. 12, Corolla • (252) 453-4484

Portsmouth Island ATV Excursions
N.C. Hwy. 12, Ocracoke Village • (252) 928-4484

Athletic Clubs

Despite all the outdoor activities the Outer Banks has to offer, many locals and visitors still crave vigorous indoor workouts at traditional gyms and health clubs. These fitness centers are open year round and include locker room and shower facilities. They are open to the public for annual, monthly, weekly and walk-in daily membership rates.

Sanderling Inn Resort Health Club
N.C Hwy. 12, Sanderling • (252) 255-0870, (252) 449-6656

Barrier Island Fitness Center
U.S. Hwy. 158, MP 1, Kitty Hawk • (252) 261-0100

Outer Banks Nautilus Athletic Club
N.C. Hwy. 12, MP 7, Kill Devil Hills • (252) 441-7001

Nautics Hall Health & Fitness Complex
U.S. Hwy. 64, Manteo • (252) 473-1191

Frisco Fitness Works
N.C. Hwy. 12, Frisco • (252) 995-3900

Biking and Skating

With two lanes of N.C. Hwy. 12 stretching along more than 100 miles of blacktop from Corolla to Ocracoke, and hugging the seaside almost all the way, cyclists and in-line skaters can cruise throughout the Outer Banks and get almost anywhere they want to go. The flat terrain on these barrier islands makes the area perfect even for beginners. Three off-road, paved paths on Roanoke Island and in South Nags Head and Kill Devil Hills provide safer routes for everyone to follow. Also, Wheels of Dare bicycle club schedules sporadic tours and treks throughout the year; call Charles Hardy at (252) 473-3328 daytime or (252) 441-3805 at night.

Kill Devil Hills and Nags Head restrict in-line skating along U.S. Highway 158 and the Beach Road. But there's a wonderful bike path near the Wright Memorial off Colington Road that winds behind the monument and connects up to another path behind First Flight Village in Kill Devil Hills. You're also allowed to use paths in the memorial, where you can ride or skate for miles. It's a good idea to check the rules with each town before putting your wheels on the asphalt.

Ocean Atlantic Rentals
Corolla Light Village Shops, N.C. Hwy. 12, Corolla • (252) 453-2440
N.C. Hwy. 12, Duck • (252) 261-4346
N.C. Hwy. 12, MP 10, Nags Head • (252) 441-7823
N.C. Hwy. 12, Avon • (252) 995-5868

Kitty Hawk Kites/Outer Banks Outdoors
N.C. Hwy. 12, Corolla • (252) 453-3685
U.S. Hwy. 158, MP 13, Nags Head • (252) 441-4124
The Waterfront, Manteo • (252) 473-2357
Hatteras Landing, Hatteras • (252) 986-1446, (800) 334-4777

The Bike Barn
Monteray Plaza, N.C. Hwy. 12, Corolla • (252) 453-0788
1312 Wrightsville Blvd., Kill Devil Hills • (252) 441-3786
N.C. Hwy. 12, Hatteras Village • (252) 986-BIKE

KDH Cycle and Skate
Sea Holly Square, N.C. Hwy 12, MP 9½, Kill Devil Hills • (252) 480-3399

Family Life Center
U.S. Hwy. 158, MP 11½, Nags Head • (252) 441-4941

Kitty Hawk Sports
U.S. Hwy. 158, MP 13, Nags Head • (225) 441-6800

Island Cycles
N.C. Hwy. 12, Avon • (252) 995-4336, (800) 229-7810

Photo: Courtesy of Georgia Beach

Parasail and soar with the gulls over the Outer Banks.

Hatteras Wind & Surf
N.C. Hwy. 12, Avon • (252) 995-6257

Lee Robinson's General Store
N.C. Hwy. 12, Hatteras Village • (252) 986-2381

Slushy Stand
N.C. Hwy. 12, Ocracoke Village • (252) 928-1878

Island Rentals
Silver Lake Rd., Ocracoke Village • (252) 928-5480

Beach Outfitters
N.C. Hwy. 12, Ocracoke Village • (252) 928-6261, (252) 928-7411

Bowling

Sometimes even the most dedicated sun-worshippers need an afternoon or evening in air-conditioned comfort. When you've caught too many rays or the weather just won't cooperate, bowling is an alternative way to wile away the hours on the Outer Banks.

Nags Head Bowling
U.S. Hwy. 158, MP 10, Nags Head • (252) 441-7077

Climbing

Sport climbing walls are available at the following locations.

Kitty Hawk Kites/Outer Banks Outdoors
Monteray Plaza, N.C. Hwy. 12, Corolla • (252) 453-3685
TimBuck II, N.C. Hwy 12, Corolla • (252) 453-8845
U.S. Hwy 158, MP 13, Nags Head • (252) 441-4124
Hatteras Landing, N.C. Hwy. 12, Hatteras Village • (252) 986-1446

Dolphin Tours, Boat Rides and Pirate Trips

Most Outer Banks boat cruises are included in our Watersports and Fishing chapters. However, a few unusual offerings are worth mentioning here as well. These trips, of course, are weather-dependent and available only during warmer spring and summer months. Reservations are recommended for each of these tours. Unlike sailing and more participatory water adventures, you don't have to be able to swim to enjoy these activities and you probably won't even get wet on board these boats that slip along the shallow sounds.

The Waterworks
U.S. Hwy. 158, MP 17, Nags Head • (252) 441-8875

Willett's Wetsports
Caribbean Corners, Nags Head/Manteo Cswy., Nags Head • (252) 441-4112, (252) 473-1748

The Crystal Dawn
Pirate's Cove Marina, Manteo • (252) 473-5577

Captain Johnny
Queen Elizabeth St., Manteo • (252) 473-1475

Downeast Rover
Manteo Waterfront Marina, Manteo • (252) 473-4866

Captain Clam
N.C. Hwy. 12, Hatteras Village • (252) 986-2460

The Windfall
The Community Store, N.C. Hwy. 12, Ocracoke Village • (252) 928-7245

Go-carts

If you're looking for a way to race around the Outer Banks without fear of getting a ticket, several go-cart rental outlets offer riders a thrill a minute on exciting, curving tracks. Drivers have to be at least 12 years old to take the wheel at most of these places, but younger children are often allowed to strap themselves in beside adults to experience the fast-paced action.

Corolla Raceway
N.C. Hwy. 12, Corolla • (252) 453-9100

Colington Speedway
1064 Colington Rd., Kill Devil Hills • (252) 480-9144

Dowdy's Go-Karts
N.C. Hwy 12, MP 11, Nags Head • (252) 441-5122

Dowdy's Amusement Park
U.S. Hwy. 158, MP 11, Nags Head • (252) 441-5122

Speed-n-Spray Action Park
U.S. Hwy. 158, MP 15, Nags Head • (252) 480-1900

Nags Head Raceway
U.S. Hwy. 158, MP 16, Nags Head • (252) 480-4639

Waterfall Park
N.C. Hwy. 12, Rodanthe • (252) 987-2213

Golf

Challenge. Variety. Beauty.

If that doesn't hook you on the Outer Banks golf experience you might want to retire your clubs. OK, we admit that most golf courses in general have a certain lushness if they're well-maintained, but how many can boast pristine natural settings including soundside views, dunescapes and teasing glimpses of the ocean? Couple Mother Nature's contributions with the artificial creations and the Outer Banks golfer will experience a peaceful respite with variety in layouts, club atmosphere and prices. Whether choosing to wander a lush soundside course or practice on a putting green, amateurs and pros alike can find something here to satisfy their golfing needs.

Courses are spread from the Currituck County mainland and Corolla south to Hatteras Island. We've included an excellent Hertford course that's only an hour drive from the Outer Banks. It's a good idea to check periodically for any new courses sprouting up because golf on the Outer Banks is spreading like wildfire. Look for a brand new club opening in July 1998 in Grandy. We haven't tested the course, but it is owned by the same folks who own The Pointe Golf Club that we note in this chapter. The Carolina Club will be on U.S. Highway 158, sporting 7000 yards and five sets of tees. A residential area will be developed around the course.

Check out our course listings. All the regulation courses are semiprivate (the general public may pay and play), and all welcome beginners and newcomers as well as seasoned low handicappers.

Regulation and Executive Courses

Currituck Club
N.C. Hwy. 12, Corolla • (252) 453-9400, (888) 453-9400

Duck Woods Country Club
50 Dogwood Tr., Kitty Hawk • (252) 261-2609

Goose Creek Golf and Country Club
U.S. Hwy. 158, Grandy •(252) 453-4008, (800) 443-4008

Nags Head Golf Links
5615 S. Seachase Dr., Nags Head • (252) 441-8073, (800) 851-9404

Ocean Edge Golf Course
Off N.C. Hwy. 12, Frisco • (252) 995-4100

The Pointe Golf Club
U.S. Hwy. 158 E., Powells Point • (252) 491-8388

Sea Scape Golf Links
300 Eckner St., Kitty Hawk • (252) 261-2158

The Sound Golf Links
101 Clubhouse Dr., Hertford • (252) 426-5555, (800) 535-0704

Hang Gliding

The closest any human being will ever get to feeling like a bird is by flying beneath the brightly colored wings of a hang glider, with arms and legs outstretched and only the wind all around. Lessons are available for flight of all ages. Just watching these winged creatures soar atop Jockey's Ridge or catching air lifts above breakers along the Atlantic is enough to make bystanders want to test their wings.

Kitty Hawk Kites/Outer Banks Outdoors
U.S. Hwy. 158, MP 13, Nags Head • (252) 441-4124, (800) 334-3777

Horseback Riding

Our favorite way to experience the Outer Banks is without gasoline or motors — on the back of a gentle horse clopping through the sand. Some folks in Kitty Hawk and Wanchese villages keep their own horses for private rides, and we envy their freedom to roam these barrier islands on the backs of such majestic animals. Even if you don't own your own horse, you can still enjoy riding one. Year-round trips are offered on Hatteras Island, and seasonal sojourns near sea and sound are available on Ocracoke.

Buxton Stables
N.C. Hwy. 12, Buxton • (252) 995-4659

Seaside Stables
N.C. Hwy. 12, Ocracoke • (252) 928-3778

Miniature Golf Courses

No beach vacation is complete unless you putt a brightly colored ball through a windmill, under a pirate's sword or across a slightly sloping hill into a small metal cup. On the Outer Banks, more than a dozen minigolf courses await fun-loving families and friends from Corolla through Hatteras Island. Themed fairways featuring African animals, circus clowns and strange obstacles await even the most amateur club-swinging families. Small children will enjoy the ease of some of these holes, and even skilled golfers can get into the new par 3 grass courses that have been growing in numbers over recent years.

You can tee off at most places by 10 AM. Many courses stay open past midnight for night owls to enjoy. Several of these attractions offer play-all-day packages for a single price. Almost all minigolf courses operate seasonally, and, since they are all outside, their openings are weather-dependent.

The Grass Course
N.C. Hwy 12, Corolla • (252) 453-4198

The Promenade
U.S. Hwy. 158, MP ¼, Kitty Hawk • (252) 261-4900

Bermuda Greens
U.S. Hwy. 158 and N.C. Hwy. 12, MP 1¼, Kitty Hawk • (252) 261-0101

The Grass Course
U.S. Hwy. 158, MP 5½, Kitty Hawk • (252) 441-7626

Lost Treasure Golf
U.S. Hwy. 158, MP 7¼, Kill Devil Hills • (252) 480-0142

Diamond Shoals Family Fun Park
U.S. Hwy. 158, MP 9¾, Kill Devil Hills • (252) 480-3553

Pink Elephant Mini Golf
N.C. Hwy. 12, MP 11, Nags Head • (252) 441-5875

Blackbeard's Miniature Golf Park
U.S. Hwy. 158, MP 15, Nags Head • (252) 441-4541

Jurassic Putt
U.S. Hwy. 158, MP 16, Nags Head • (252) 441-6841

Avon Golf
N.C. Hwy. 12, Avon • (252) 995-5480

Cool Wave Ice Cream Shop and Miniature Golf
N.C. Hwy. 12, Buxton • (252) 995-6366

Parasailing

If you've always wanted to float high above the water, beneath a colorful parachute, opportunities for such peaceful adventures await you at a variety of locations along the Outer Banks. This is one of the most enjoyable experiences we've had during summer. Our only regrets are that the incredible rides don't last longer. We could stay up at these lofty heights, strapped comfortably into a climbing harness, swinging beneath billowing air-filled chutes for hours.

Although a boat pulls you from below, allowing the wind to lift you toward the clouds, you don't get wet on these outdoor adventures over the sounds unless you want to. Riders don't even have to know how to swim to soar with the sea gulls above whitecaps and beach cottages. Anyone of any age, without any athletic ability at all, will enjoy parasailing and find it one of their most memorable pastimes. And it's safe too. Unbreakable ropes are standard.

Kitty Hawk Watersports
N.C. Hwy. 12, Corolla • (252) 453-6900

Above It All Parasail
1446 Duck Rd., Duck • (252) 261-4200

North Beach Sailing
N.C. Hwy. 12, Duck • (252) 261-7100

The Waterworks
N.C. Hwy. 12, Duck • (252) 261-7245
U.S. Hwy. 158, MP 17, Nags Head • (252) 441-8875

Nags Head Watersports
Nags Head/Manteo Cswy., Nags Head • (252) 480-2236

Island Parasail
N.C. Hwy. 12, Avon • (252) 995-4970

Tennis

Many cottage rental developments throughout the Outer Banks have private tennis courts for their guests. Outdoor public tennis courts are located near the Kill Devil Hills Fire Station, at the Baum Senior Center in Kill Devil Hills, behind Kelly's Restaurant in Nags Head, at Manteo Middle School, at Manteo High School and next to Cape Hatteras School in Buxton. If you don't own a racquet, or left yours back on the mainland, you can lease one by the day or week from Ocean Atlantic Rentals in Corolla, (252) 453-2440; Duck, (252) 261-4346; Nags Head, (252) 441-7823; or Avon, (252) 995-5868.

Pine Island Racquet Club
N.C. Hwy. 12, Duck • (252) 453-8525

Waterslides, Arcades and Other Amusements

On those hot afternoons when you're ready for a break from sand and saltwater, slip on down to a waterslide, and splash into one of their big pools. Most of these parks are open daily during the summer — some well into the evening. Waterslides generally close on rainy days.

Among the recreational outposts, many include video arcades with their offerings, but the Outer Banks' oldest and newest amusement centers also offer bright computerized games and other unusual activities. We can't list everything the owners of these establishments include, so you'll have to experience these places for yourself to discover all the surprises in store.

Diamond Shoals Family Fun Park
U.S. Hwy. 158, MP 9¾, Kill Devil Hills • (252) 480-3553

Surf Slide
U.S. 158, MP 10, Nags Head • (252) 441-5755

Village Playhouse
105 Mall Dr., Nags Head • (252) 441-3277

Capt. Marty's
U.S Hwy. 158, MP 14½, Nags Head • (252) 441-3132

Waterfall Action Park
N.C. Hwy. 12, Rodanthe • (252) 987-2213

Watersports

With about 900 square miles of water in Dare County alone, visitors and residents can — and do — take full advantage of the range of opportunities to play in and on the pristine waterways that dominant this unique strand of islands. Surfing and windsurfing are among the area's most popular watersports. Personal watercraft, including Jet Skis, Sea Doos and Waverunners, have also exploded in popularity, with rental outposts opening all along the sound shores.

Kayaking, canoeing and sailing also are more available, as ecotours and sunset cruises become increasingly popular pastimes. For more unusual endeavors, the National Park Service offers occasional snorkeling expeditions for families. Some Outer Banks surf shops have begun leasing skimboards to daredevils who like to skirt the shoreline breakers. A few marinas along the barrier islands are even renting powerboats for near-shore fishing and water-skiing.

What makes water activities on these waterlogged barrier islands so attractive is that every person, whether an athletic adventurer or a couch potato, can have exactly what they want. Generally, you'll have fun sharing the wet wonderlands with the fish and birds — and scores of other water lovers who are just as thrilled as you are to be part of the Outer Banks water scene.

Surfing

Warmer than New England waters and wielding more consistent waves than most Florida beaches, the Outer Banks are reputed to have the best surf breaks on the East Coast. Local surfing experts explain that since we are set out farther into the ocean in deeper waters than other coastal regions, our beaches pick up more swells and wind patterns than any place around. Piers, shipwrecks and offshore sandbars also create unusual wave patterns.

The beaches from Duck through Hatteras are some of the only spots left that don't have strict surfing regulations: As long as you keep a leash on your board and stay at least 300 feet away from public piers, you won't get a surfing citation.

Cape Hatteras' black-and-white striped lighthouse, set in the elbow of the barrier islands, had become known as a magnet for East Coast swell seekers by the early 1970s. Jim Vaughn opened one of the Outer Banks' first surf stores at Whalebone Junction in Nags Head in 1975. Today, more than 20 shops can be found up and down the barrier islands.

Surfers at shops along the barrier islands design, shape and sell their own boards, with prices ranging from $100 for used models to $600 for custom styles. Some stores offer lessons for beginning surfers, and many rent boards for as little as $10 a day plus a deposit. Don't forget board wax, or you won't be riding very long!

Surfing is a strenuous sport, and you need to be able to swim well in wicked waves, but with a variety of board lengths — and 90 miles of oceanfront to choose from — there are usually breaks to accommodate almost every surfer's style and stamina.

Since the beaches have been getting increasingly crowded with summer surfers, some folks won't reveal favorite spots to catch waves. We'll share some of the best-known haunts with you here, though: Kitty Hawk Pier and Avalon Pier in Kill Devil Hills each boast ample parking and pretty rideable waves. The public beach access at Barnes Street in Nags Head, with plenty of parking, provides some steady swells. Nags Head Pier also is a favorite spot. If you don't mind hiking across the dunes with a board under your arm, Pea Island and Coquina Beach both have waves worth the walk. Rodanthe has always been a popular destination, with the pier there producing waves even when almost everything else around is flat. Ramp 34, just north of Avon, is another good location, as are the turnout north of Buxton, Ramp 49 in Frisco, Frisco Pier and the public beach access area between Frisco and Hatteras Village.

The best and biggest waves by far, however, roll in around the Cape Hatteras Lighthouse. Here, beaches north and south of Cape Point, which juts closest to the Gulf Stream, face in two directions, doubling the chances for good conditions. Concrete and steel groins jut out into the Atlantic near the beacon's brick base though, so beware of being tossed toward one of these head-bashing barriers.

Surf's up!

Surf Shops

Ranging from sublime to specialized to hip, the Outer Banks is inundated with surf shops. And the shops are the hotspots for wave riders of all ages and skill levels. Each summer, surf shop managers post competition schedules for beginners through surfing-circuit riders near the storefronts. Most shops stock gear, and many offer instruction during the season. Following are some favorites of Outer Banks' surfers.

Corolla Surf Shop
Corolla Light Village Shops, 110-A Austin Dr., Corolla • (252) 453-WAVE
TimBuck II Shopping Village, N.C. Hwy. 12, Corolla • (252) 453-9273

Wave Riding Vehicles
U.S. Hwy. 158, MP 2, Kitty Hawk • (252) 261-7952

Whalebone Surfshop
U.S Hwy. 158, MP 2, Kitty Hawk • (252) 261-8737
U.S. Hwy. 158, MP 10, Nags Head • (252) 441-6747

Watermans Class Longboards-Surf Boutique
Cooke's Corner, U.S. Hwy. 158, MP 6, Kill Devil Hills • (252) 449-0459

The Vitamin Sea
U.S. Hwy. 158, MP 6, Kill Devil Hills • (252) 441-7512

The Pit Surf Hangout
U.S. Hwy. 158, MP 9, Kill Devil Hills • (252) 480-3128

The Secret Spot
U.S Hwy. 158, MP 11, Nags Head • (252) 441-4030

Rodanthe Surf Shop
N.C. Hwy. 12, Rodanthe • (252) 987-2412

Hatteras Island Surf Shop
N.C. Hwy. 12, Waves • (252) 987-2296

Natural Art Surf Shop
N.C. Hwy. 12, Buxton • (252) 995-5682

Hatteras Wind & Surf
N.C. Hwy. 12, Avon • (252) 995-6275, (888) 963-SURF

Ride The Wind Surf Shop
N.C. Hwy. 12, Ocracoke • (252) 928-6311

Windsurfing

Since the early 1980s, windsurfing has grown from a relatively obscure sport to one of the most popular activities on the Outer Banks. Each year, especially in autumn, thousands of northern visitors descend on the barrier islands to skim the shallow sounds or surf the sea's whitecaps on brightly colored sailboards. When the wind is whipping just right, hundreds of neon-striped sails soar along the shores of Hatteras Island, silently skirting the salty water like bright butterflies flitting near the beach.

Whether you're an expert athlete or novice who knows nothing about wind and water, windsurfing is not an easy sport. Once you get the hang of it, however, it is one of the most intoxicating experiences imaginable. It's clean and quiet.

Canadian Hole, on the west side of N.C. 12 between Avon and Buxton, is undoubtedly the most popular windsurfing spot on the Outer Banks and the East Coast. Formed in the early 1960s, it was created after a storm cut an inlet across Hatteras Island, just north of Buxton, and workers dredged sand from the sound to rebuild the roadway. Dredging activities carved troughs just offshore in the Pamlico Sound. The deep depressions, which extend to about 5 feet, help create ideal conditions for sailboarders. Additionally, Canadian Hole flanks one of the skinniest strips of sand on the barrier islands. Windsurfers can sail the sound and then walk their boards across N.C. 12 to cruise in the ocean in fewer than five minutes.

Nags Head's soundside beaches also provide great sailboarding. The sounds are more shallow than Canadian Hole, thus safer for beginners. In spring and fall, tourism officials estimate, as many as 500 windsurfers a week arrive at the Outer Banks. Dozens of other visitors try the sport for the first time while vacationing in Dare County.

Windsurfing Shops

Whether you're looking for a lesson, need a sail of a different size or want to ask for advice about sailboarding, more than a dozen

Photo: Courtesy of J. Aaron Trotman

You can boogie board, skim board or surf until you drop.

shops from Corolla through Ocracoke stock windsurfing supplies, and many provide instructors in season.

Barrier Island Boats
N.C. Hwy. 12, Duck • (252) 261-7100

Kitty Hawk Watersports
U.S Hwy. 158, MP 16, Nags Head • (252) 441-2756

Hatteras Island Sail Shop
N.C. Hwy 12, Waves • (252) 987-2292

Windsurfing Hatteras
N.C. Hwy. 12, Avon • (252) 995-4970

Hatteras Wind & Surf
N.C. Hwy. 12, Avon • (252) 995-6275

Kayaking and Canoeing

The easiest, most adaptable and accessible watersports available on the Outer Banks — kayaking and canoeing — are activities people of any age or physical ability can enjoy. These lightweight paddlecrafts are extremely maneuverable, can glide almost anywhere along the seas or sounds and afford adventurous activity as well as silent solitude. They're also relatively inexpensive ways to tour uncharted waterways and see sights you'd miss if you stayed on shore.

Paddling Places

All the sounds around the Outer Banks are ideal for kayaking and canoeing, because they are shallow, warm and filled with flora and fauna. There are marked trails at Alligator River National Wildlife Refuge; buoys around Wanchese, Manteo and Colington; and plenty of uncharted areas to explore around Pine Island, Pea Island, Kitty Hawk, Corolla and the Cape Hatteras National Seashore. Unlike other types of boats, you don't even need a special launching site to set a kayak or canoe in the water and take off.

Corolla Outback Adventures
Wee Winks Shopping Center, N.C Hwy. 12, Corolla • (252) 453-4484

Barrier Island Boats
N.C. Hwy. 12, Duck • (252) 261-7100

Outer Banks Outdoors
U.S. Hwy. 158, Nags Head • (252) 441-4124, (800) 334-4777

Kitty Hawk Kayaks
U.S Hwy. 158, MP 13, Nags Head • (252) 441-6800

Wilderness Canoeing Inc.
Melvin T. Twiddy Jr., P.O. Box 789, Manteo, NC 27954 • (252) 473-1960

Hatteras Wind & Surf
N.C. Hwy. 12, Avon • (252) 995-6275

Kayaking Hatteras
N.C. Hwy. 12, Avon • (252) 995-3033

Ocracoke Adventures
N.C. Hwy. 12 and Silver Lake Rd., Ocracoke Village • (252) 928-7873

Ride The Wind Surf Shop
N.C. Hwy. 12, Ocracoke Village • (252) 928-6311

Scuba Diving

Cloudier and cooler than waters off the Florida Keys and the Caribbean Islands, offshore areas along the Outer Banks offer unique scuba-diving experiences in "The Graveyard of the Atlantic." More than 500 shipwrecks, at least 200 named and identified, are strewn along the sand from Corolla to Ocracoke. Experienced divers enjoy the challenge of unpredictable currents and always seem to find something new to explore beneath the ocean's surface. From 17th-century schooners to World War II submarines, wreckage lies at a variety of depths, in almost every imaginable condition. After each storm, it seems, a new shipwreck is unearthed somewhere near the barrier island shores. Many of these wrecks haven't been seen since they sank beneath the sea.

Some underwater archaeological shipwreck sites are federally protected and can be visited — but not touched. Others offer incredible souvenirs for deepwater divers: bits of china plates and teacups, old medicine and liquor bottles, even brass-rimmed port-hole covers and thick, hand-blown glass that's been buried beneath the ocean for more than a century. If you prefer to leave history as you find it, waterproof cameras are sure to bring back even more memorable treasures from the mostly unexplored underwater world.

Some dive shops can also recommend shallow dive spots that you don't need a boat to get to as well as near shore or sound areas you can explore with just a face mask and snorkel. Ocean Atlantic Rentals in Corolla, (252) 453-2440, and Avon, (252) 995-5868, rents fins, masks and snorkels. Ride the Wind Surf Shop, on Ocracoke

Island, (252) 928-6311, offers an afternoon snorkeling trip daily in season. And the National Park Service also offers sporadic snorkeling adventures along the Cape Hatteras National Seashore in the summer. Call (252) 473-2111 for tour times and information.

Dive Shops

Sea Scan Dive Centre
N.C. Hwy. 12, MP 10, Nags Head • (252) 480-3467

Nags Head Pro Dive Center
Surfside Plaza, U.S. Hwy. 158, MP 13½, Nags Head • (252) 441-7594

Diamond Shoals Diving
52346 N.C. Hwy. 12, Frisco • (252) 995-4021

Sailing

With wide, shallow sounds and more than 90 miles of easily accessible oceanfront, the Outer Banks has been a haven for sailors since Sir Walter Raleigh's explorers first slid along these shores more than four centuries ago. Private sailboat owners have long enjoyed the barrier islands as a stopover en route along the Intracoastal Waterway.

Until recently, you had to have your own sailboat to cruise the area waterways. Now, dozens of shops from Corolla through Ocracoke rent sailboats, Hobie Cats and catamarans to weekend water bugs. Others offer introductory and advanced sailing lessons. Some even take people who have no desire to learn to sail on excursions across the sounds aboard multi-passenger sailing ships. Ecotours, luncheon swim-and-sails and sunset cruises have become increasingly popular with vacationers who want to glide across the waterways but not necessarily steer their own vessels.

Sailboat Cruises, Courses and Rentals

Prices for sailboat cruises depend on the amenities, length of voyage and time of day. Midday trips sometimes include boxed lunches or at least drinks for passengers. Some sunset tours offer parties wine, beer and appetizers. Almost all of the excursions let people bring their own food and drink aboard, and some even accept dogs on leashes aboard the decks. Special arrangements can also be made for handicapped passengers. Prices generally range from $30 to $60 per person. Some captains will also offer their services along with the sailboats, beginning at $50 per hour per vessel, and allowing the renter to fill the craft with its capacity of passengers.

Lesson costs, too, span a range, depending on how in-depth the course is, what type of craft you're learning on and whether you prefer group or individualized instruction. Costs can be from $10 to $50 per person. Call ahead for group rates if you've got more than four people in your party.

If you'd rather rent a craft and sail it yourself, dozens of Outer Banks outfitters lease sailboats by the hour, day or week. Deposits generally are required. Costs range from $25 to $60 per hour and $50 to $110 per day. Most shops accept major credit cards.

Barrier Island Boats
N.C. Hwy. 12, Duck • (252) 261-7100

Promenade Watersports
U.S Hwy. 158, MP ¼, Kitty Hawk • (252) 261-4400

The Waterworks
U.S. Hwy. 158, MP 16½, Nags Head • (252) 441-8875

Outer Banks Outdoors
Queen Elizabeth St., Manteo • (252) 473-2357, (800) 334-4777
Atlantic Estates, N.C. Hwy. 12, Avon • (252) 995-6060

Island Sail
The Waterfront, Manteo • (252) 473-1213

Hatteras Island Sail Shop
N.C. Hwy. 12, Waves • (252) 987-2292

Hatteras Watersports
N.C. Hwy. 12, Salvo • (252) 987-2306

Avon Watersports
N.C. Hwy. 12, Avon • (252) 995-4970

Boating

From small skiffs to luxurious pleasure boats, there is dock space for almost every type of boat on the Outer Banks. Most marinas require advance reservations. Space is extremely limited on summer weekends, so call as soon as you make plans to visit the area. Prices vary greatly, depending on the dock location, amenities and type of vessel you're operating.

If you're not lucky enough to own your own boat, you can still access the sounds, inlets and ocean around the Outer Banks by renting powerboats from area outfitters. Most store owners don't require previous boating experience. If you leave a deposit and driver's license, they'll include a brief boating lesson in the rental price. Whether you're looking to lease a craft to catch this evening's fish dinner or just want to take the kids on an afternoon cruise, you can find a vessel to suit your needs at a variety of marinas. Prices range from $15 an hour to more than $100 per day, depending on the type of boat. Some places require a two-hour or more minimum. Most accept major credit cards.

Marinas, Dock Space
and Public Launch Ramps

If you just need a place to put your boat in the water, you'll find free public launch ramps on the soundside end of Wampum Drive in Duck; on Kitty Hawk Bay in Kitty Hawk; at the end of Soundside Road, behind Jockey's Ridge State Park in Nags Head; below the Washington Baum Bridge between Nags Head and Manteo; near Thicket Lump Lane in Wanchese; at the oceanside end of Lighthouse Road in Buxton; and on the sound in Ocracoke Village.

Pirate's Cove Yacht Club
Manteo-Nags Head Cswy., Manteo • (252) 473-3906, (800) 367-4728

Manteo Waterfront Marina
207 Queen Elizabeth Ave., Ste. 14, Manteo • (252) 473-3320, (888) 473-BOAT

Salty Dawg Marina
U.S Hwy. 64, Manteo • (252) 473-3405

Thicket Lump Marina
Thicket Lump Rd., Wanchese • (252) 473-4500

Frisco Cove Marina
N.C. Hwy. 12, Frisco • (252) 995-4242

Hatteras Harbor Marina
N.C. Hwy. 12 and Gulfstream Way, Hatteras Village • (252) 986-2166

Willis Boat Landing
N.C. Hwy. 12, Hatteras Village • (252) 986-2208

Oden's Dock
N.C. Hwy. 12, Hatteras Village • (252) 986-2555

Teach's Lair Marina
N.C. Hwy. 12, Hatteras Village • (252) 986-2460

The National Park Service Dock
Silver Lake, Ocracoke Village • (252) 928-5111

Boat Rentals

If you don't own a powerboat but want to explore the vast waters of this region, you can rent a boat. Lots of places, even marinas or rent-all services, will often rent boats. Following are some reliable sources if you're looking for motorboats.

Barrier Island Boats
N.C. Hwy. 12, Duck • (252) 261-7100

Waterworks Too
N.C. Hwy. 12, Duck • (252) 261-7245

North Duck Watersports
N.C. Hwy. 12, Duck • (252) 261-4200

Promenade Watersports
U.S. Hwy. 158, MP ¼, Kitty Hawk • (252) 261-4400

Nags Head Watersports
Nags Head/Manteo Cswy., Nags Head • (252) 480-2236

The Waterworks
U.S Hwy. 158, MP 16½, Nags Head • (252) 441-8875

Hatteras Jack Inc.
N.C. Hwy. 12, Rodanthe • (252) 987-2428

Frisco Cove Marina
N.C. Hwy. 12, Frisco • (252) 995-4242

Island Rentals
Silver Lake Rd., Ocracoke Village • (252) 928-5480

Personal Watercraft

If you feel a need for speed and enjoy the idea of riding a motor-cycle across the water, more than a dozen Outer Banks outposts rent personal watercraft by the hour. No experience is necessary to ride these powerful boat-like devices, although a training session is a must if you've never before piloted a personal watercraft. Unlike landlocked go-carts and other speedy road rides, there aren't any lanes to stick to on the open sound or ocean.

Personal watercraft are akin to motorboats with inboard mo-tors that power a water pump. There aren't any propellers or out-side engine parts, so fingers and toes generally stay safe. Like other motorized boats, however, personal watercraft are loud and can be dangerous if you don't know what you're doing. Most rental outposts include brief instructions and sometimes even a video on how to handle Waverunners, Jet Skis and Runabouts.

Renting Personal Watercraft

Shops from Corolla to Hatteras Island rent personal watercraft beginning at $30 a half-hour. Price wars occasionally will result in the cost being slashed to rock bottom. Regardless, more powerful models are generally more expensive. Additional charges also some-times apply for extra riders on the Waverunners. Personal water-craft also can be rented by the hour, day or even week at some spots.

Corolla Watersports at the Inn at Corolla Lighthouse
1066 Ocean Tr., Corolla • (252) 453-8602

Kitty Hawk Watersports
N.C. Hwy. 12, Corolla • (252) 453-6900

North Duck Watersports
N.C. Hwy. 12, Duck • (252) 261-4200

Barrier Island Boats
N.C. Hwy. 12, Duck • (252) 261-7100

Promenade Watersports
U.S Hwy. 158, MP ¼, Kitty Hawk • (252) 261-4400

The Waterworks
U.S. Hwy. 158, MP 16½, Nags Head • (252) 441-8875

Nags Head Water Sports
Nags Head/Manteo Cswy., Nags Head • (252) 480-2236

Willett's Wetsports
Nags Head/Manteo Cswy., Nags Head • (252) 441-4112

Hatteras Watersports
N.C. Hwy. 12, Salvo • (252) 987-2306

Frisco Cove Marina
N.C. Hwy. 12, Frisco • (252) 995-4242

Photo: Courtesy of the Dare County Tourist Bureau

This proud Outer Banks angler displays his catch.

Fishing

If you haven't already heard through the grapevine about our infamous Outer Banks fishing, you're in for a treat. The diversity of fish available in the waters here makes this area a hot spot for anglers from far and wide. Charter boats leave the docks year round for offshore waters teeming with big game fish. The inlets, sounds, rivers and lakes abound with saltwater and freshwater species, and surf-casters and pier anglers have plenty of opportunities to catch a variety of fish from the shell-fringed beaches or wooden planks that hover over the sea and sounds. Whether you're a novice or a pro, angling with heavy or light tackle for food or for sport, the Outer Banks is a world-class fishing center — and we can prove this boast by checking the International Game Fish Association World Record Game Fishes listings.

Many record-breaking fish have been caught here — both offshore and inshore — including the all-tackle record for blue marlin (1,142 pounds) in 1974, and the all-tackle world-record bluefish (31 pounds, 12 ounces), caught off Hatteras in 1972. And then there was that world-record red drum caught off Avon, a record-breaking Spanish mackerel caught in Ocracoke Inlet, a lemon shark caught off Buxton and a scalloped hammerhead shark landed off Cape Point. Let's not leave out an oyster toadfish and a myriad of saltwater fly-rod and saltwater-line class world-record catches.

You might think, "the variety draws expert anglers, hence the great catches." Well, there's more to the story. Chances of a good catch are enhanced by physical conditions existing here that you won't find anywhere else. And that ain't no fish story! Stay tuned. We outline these characteristics in our offshore section below.

Another factor that influences the catch is that the Outer Banks has multiple experienced charter fleets with mates on board to show you the ropes. Getting a job as a mate on a charter boat is no simple matter — the competition to work these famous waters is fierce.

While anyone who's gone fishing knows you can't predict catching fish, they'll be guided by charter boat captains who know what species should be in the area and who will help you make wise choices on the morning of the trip. Charters leave the docks for inshore and offshore fishing every day that the weather permits. When you call to book a boat (see our Marinas listings in this chapter), you may find it hard to know what kind of trip to choose unless you've fished before. Booking agents at each marina will guide you.

In the following sections, we describe offshore and inshore angling, backwater, surf, fly and pier fishing. Offshore trips generally leave the docks at 5:30 AM and return no later than 6 PM. Inshore trips are half-day excursions that leave twice daily, generally at 7 AM and again around noon. Intermediate trips can last all day but generally don't travel as far as the Gulf Stream.

We're certain you'll have a pleasant adventure no matter how far out you venture. If you're taking out your own boat, it's important to get information on size limits, creel limits and season dates. You don't want to risk getting a fine by bringing in too small or too many restricted fish. Check with any tackle shop, or call the North Carolina Division of Marine Fisheries at (800) 682-2632 for this kind of information. For information on freshwater licenses, check the regulations digest published by the North Carolina Wildlife Resources Commission. It's available at sporting-goods stores and tackle shops. Official weigh stations are listed toward the end of this chapter.

Offshore Fishing

The majority of Outer Banks captains who lead you to offshore fishing grounds have been working these waters for years. Many are second- and third-generation watermen. They generally choose the daily fishing spot depending on recent trends, seasons and weather. Occasionally, when there's a slow spell, a captain will move away from the rest of the fleet to play out a hunch. If the maverick meets with success, it's common for him/her to share this find with the rest of the fleet. In other words, our area boasts of a brother- or sisterhood that visiting anglers say they've experienced nowhere else. This camaraderie can't help but enhance the fishing experience, plus, fishing together is safer.

Anglers fishing offshore for big game fish generally troll (drag fishing lines behind the moving boat). If you run into a school of fish, such as dolphin (mahi mahi), the captain will stop the boat so the party can cast into the water that's been primed with chum, or fish bits. Chumming also is used on bluefin tuna trips. All these techniques are explained the day of the trip. Expect to pay about $950 for six people to charter an offshore fishing excursion. Bluefin tuna trips are higher, costing between $1,000 and $12,000. Some off-shore charters go as low as $700. You have to shop around.

One offshore area that's frequented with great regularity is called The Point (not to be confused with Cape Hatteras Point). Approximately 37 miles off the Outer Banks, this primary fishing ground for local captains and mates is rich in game fish such as tuna, dolphin, wahoo, billfish and shark. Blue marlin, wahoo and dolphin show up at The Point in April and May. Yellowfin, bigeye and blackfin tuna are the anglers' mainstay year round. A significant population of yellow-fin inhabit this area in the winter, providing a tremendous seasonal fishery. You have to be patient to fish in the winter because plenty of bad weather days make traveling offshore a waiting game. If you hold out though, you can fight a deep-diving tuna.

Deep-swimming reef fish, such as grouper, snapper and tilefish, also inhabit The Point. Because of the strong current, however, you must travel a little bit south of The Point to fish for them effectively.

The Point has unique characteristics that give it a reputation for attracting and harboring a variety and quantity of fish from the minute baitfish to massive billfish (see our Natural Wonders chapter).

What also helps set this spot apart is its proximity to the edge of the Continental Shelf. Where there's a drop-off, you'll find a concentration of baitfish because of the nutrient-rich waters present and currents playing off the edge to stir things up. Anglers don't have to travel far to get to The Point since the Shelf is particularly narrow off Cape Hatteras. And The Point is the last spot where the Gulf Stream appears near the Shelf before it veers off in an east-northeasterly direction. Weather permitting, there are some days when the Gulf Stream entirely covers The Point. Other days, prevailing winds can push it farther offshore.

At about 50 miles wide and a half-mile deep, the Gulf Stream has temperatures that rarely drop below 65 to 70 degrees, providing a comfortable habitat for a variety of sea life. The Gulf Steam flows at an average rate of 2.5 mph, at times quickening to 5 mph. This steadfast flow carries away millions of tons of water per second, continually pushing along sea life in its path, including fish, micro-scopic plants and animals and gulfweed. Gulfweed lines the edge of the Gulf Stream when the winds are favorable, creating a habitat for baitfish. You can easily pull up a handful of vegetation and find it teeming with minute shrimp and fish. Anglers fish these "grass lines" as well as the warm-water eddies that spin off from the Gulf

Stream. These warm pockets, which vary in size from 20 to 100 miles long by a half-mile to a mile wide, are sometimes filled with schools of dolphin (mahi mahi), tuna and mako.

Catch-and-release fishing for bluefin tuna has anglers from across the globe traveling to Hatteras to partake in a bonanza that has really revived winter offshore charter fishing along the Outer Banks. For at least four years, captains have been noticing a massive congregation of bluefin tuna inhabiting the wrecks about 20 miles from Hatteras Inlet. We've seen the action firsthand, and the quantity of bluefin available and the frequency with which they bite are phenomenal.

Fish weighing from 200 to more than 800 pounds have been caught. These giants, which U.S. biologists say comprise an overstressed fishery in most parts of the world, are a federally protected species, so anglers almost always must release them. Restrictions state that during bluefin tuna season anglers may keep one fish from 27 to 73 inches per boat per day. The length of the tuna season is determined annually by the National Marine Fisheries and is contingent on overall poundage caught.

But just reeling in a bluefin of any magnitude will make the blood of an avid angler run hot! The bluefin seem to strike with less provocation on the choppy days — plus there aren't tons of boats flooding the area during rougher weather. On days when the fish are spooked by excessive boat traffic or simply aren't biting for whatever reason, mates will sprinkle the water with chum (choppedup fish parts, guts and blood that smells strong and draws fish) to increase the chance of a strike. These giants often jump 4 feet out of the ocean just to bite a bloody bait.

Local anglers troll, chum and use live or dead bait. We've seen great success with 130-pound test line. Some folks like to use lighter tackle for the sport of it, but the heavier the line, the better the condition of the fish when it's released. Circle hooks are also recommended for the fish's comfort — they tend to lodge in the mouth cartilage rather than in the fleshy gullet or gills.

Even though most of the fish are caught on heavy tackle, carefully handled and subsequently released, recreational charter boat captains are contemplating a self-imposed quota for catch and release to try to protect the fish even further. When there are large groups of boats present day after day, it's likely the same fish will have to do battle over and over.

Fishing parties enjoy feeding the fish and catching them on

Photo: Courtesy of Mary Ellen Riddle

Day or night, a fishing break always hits the spot.

hookless lines just to watch the strike. It's like being at a huge aquarium.

You can enjoy offshore fishing year round, but with the bluefin fishing off Hatteras, you should book a trip from January through March. Some fish may show up earlier, and there are bluefin available in early April, but by then, captains begin concentrating on yellowfin again. Bluefin boats leave the dock between 5:30 and 7 AM. You can book charters by calling any of the Outer Banks' marinas listed in this chapter. To avoid the crowds, book a weekday trip.

Offshore Headboat Fishing

Headboat fishing can give you an offshore experience without the price of chartering a boat (see our "Inshore Fishing" section on headboat fishing). Several large boats take parties — charging "by the head" — offshore all day. While you won't be targeting tuna here, you still have the chance for plentiful catches of a variety of bottom species, fine-tasting fish in their own right, including black sea bass, triggerfish, tilefish, amberjack, tautog, grouper and snapper. The species vary slightly from north to south. Occasionally small shark are hooked over the wrecks, and once in a while you'll run into some bigger game fish, but you're generally dropping a line over the side into the artificial and natural reefs or wrecks, not trolling.

The boats are open from the stern to the bow to hold anglers comfortably, and all the gear is supplied. All you have to bring is a cooler with food and drinks, sunscreen and a jacket in case the weather changes. Anglers don't need fishing licenses.

If you're venturing out in winter months, dress in layers. If you're near the Gulf Stream and the wind is blowing over it in your direction then you may be able to layer down to a T-shirt. Most of the headboats that go offshore have heat in the salon or an area that can be shut off from the cold air.

Many parents want their children to experience an offshore trip, and that's understandable. You not only fish but often get to see whales, turtles and dolphin. Our advice: Think carefully before you take a really young tyke offshore. The day is long, approximately 10 hours, and the captain doesn't turn around except in an emergency, and that does not include seasickness. The boat's deck can be slippery, and the water can be choppy. Life vests are available.

The Country Girl
Pirate's Cove Yacht Club, Nags Head-Manteo Cswy. • (252) 473-3906,
(252) 473-5577

Miss Hatteras
Oden's Dock, N.C. Hwy. 12, Hatteras Village • (252) 986-2365

Tideline Charters
Thicket Lump Marina, Thicket Lump Rd., Wanchese • (252) 261-1458

Inshore Fishing

A variety of inshore opportunities abound that will strike the fancy of the novice or expert angler. The offshore gang doesn't corner the market on fun here. Inshore generally refers to inlet, sound, lake, river and some close-range ocean fishing on a boat.

Outer Banks anglers enjoy fishing for rockfish (also called striped bass or stripers) year round. They are fun to catch and make a great tasting dinner. Though it is a regulated species, they've steadily been making a comeback during the last six years. Each year stripers spawn under the dam in Weldon, North Carolina. The young live in estuaries for several years before joining the Atlantic migratory population. A moratorium initially was placed on the fish in summer 1984, when striper stocks in the Chesapeake Bay started to decline rapidly. This was significant since about 90 percent of the Atlantic migratory stock comes from the Chesapeake Bay. Marine fisheries experts blamed overfishing and water quality for the drop. A widespread East Coast moratorium gave the species a chance to thrive again. There was a partial lifting of the moratorium in 1990, and today, while the species still is closely monitored, they afford Outer Banks anglers a hearty catch-and-release recreational fishery.

The ocean season for stripers is open year round. Anglers can keep two fish (28 inches or larger) per person per day. Though a body of stripers are present in our waters year round, the sound inhabitants are protected by restrictions. Since the sound fishing season fluctuates, the best thing to do is call your favorite tackle shop for up-to-date regulations. If you just want to catch and release, go at it anytime.

When a cold snap hits the Chesapeake Bay area, rockfish migrate down past Corolla into Oregon Inlet. November is one of the best months to fish for them around the Manns Harbor bridge that connects Roanoke Island to the East Lake community. Anglers also fish in the winter for stripers behind Roanoke Island in East and South lakes.

Stripers tend to congregate around bridge pilings. They cluster near these nutrient-covered supports that entice smaller bait fish. You can troll, use spinning tackle with lures, fly-cast or surf fish for them. Stripers are bottom feeders, so a planer can be used to catch them. If you're fishing with double hooks, once you've hooked the first fish, keep it steady in the water. Another should soon grab the second hook. Insiders suggest using a butter bean with a white bucktail on the end. You can catch them on slick calm days and in rougher weather, but a little current seems to help.

Summertime finds Outer Bankers fishing the sounds from Manteo to Ocracoke for speckled trout. Insiders suggest you move to the surf or pier to catch them in fall. The speckled trout fishing is excellent in early fall around Oregon and Hatteras inlets. They are best enjoyed on light tackle with artificial lures or on a fly rod. Light spinning tackle is another good choice. Artificial lures are the norm. Insiders suggest using a lead head jig with a soft plastic twister tail for sound, bridge and inlet fishing. For the beach, try MirrOlures. Currently the fish must be a 12-inch total length minimum to be a keeper. Call your local tackle shop for more information.

Inshore Headboat Fishing

A couple of Outer Banks' headboats ply the sounds and inlets and occasionally go several miles offshore to the wrecks on calm days. These excursions provide the perfect chance for a youngster to hold a rod, bait a hook, reel in a fish (we hope) and learn respect for wildlife. The inshore headboats are generally between 60 and 75 feet long and accommodate about 50 people. As with the offshore trips, tackle and bait are provided. We suggest you bring your own food; some headboats sell sodas and snacks, and the Miss Hatteras has a full snack bar.

Inshore headboat captains are very accommodating to families, and the mates will give you as much or as little help as you need. They'll tell you if your fish is a keeper or needs to be thrown back (some fish are not of legal size, or big enough to keep). If you're squeamish about baiting a hook or handling a fish, a mate will assist you. They seem to have a sense of when to back off and when to lend a helping hand. Half-day bottom fishing trips generally run $20 for kids and $25 for adults. Expect to bottom fish for croaker, trout, spot, flounder, sea mullet, blowtoads and pigfish; these pan-size fish are very tasty. The crew usually can identify your fish if you cannot.

Some of these headboats-by-day offer nonfishing pleasure cruises in the evenings. Many captains enjoy talking with passengers about the area's history. Local boats such as the *Miss Oregon Inlet*, *Miss Hatteras* and *Crystal Dawn* offer nonfishing excursions. Prices vary, but the average is $4 for children and $8 for adults.

A quick tip about kids on boats: Watch them carefully, and enforce a no-running code. These boats typically carry a large crowd, and not everyone will have their hooks or rod tips in the right place at the right time.

Remain positive when fishing with kids. Everywhere in the world, there are days when the fish don't bite. If you're having one of those days, let the trip be a lesson in nature, patience and people — and let your imagination roam. The adult sets the tone. A positive attitude will go far in "hooking" your little ones for life.

Small-boat Fishing

Small boats (smaller than the offshore vessels and generally in the 30-foot range) offer sound, inlet, lake, river and ocean trips that are as varied as the weather. Inshore captains generally book half-day trips but also offer intermediate all-day trips to take you farther out. If you're interested in bluefish, Spanish mackerel, cobia, king mackerel, bonito, trout, flounder, croaker and red drum, you can book trips from virtually any marina. Half-day trips are a little easier on the pocketbook.

Spanish mackerel are a mainstay of the area. Ocracoke Island captains begin looking for them in late April and typically enjoy catches through late October. Farther north on the Outer Banks, Spanish mackerel usually arrive the first or second week in May, depending on the water temperature. Casting to them is the most sporting way of catching them. We suggest you use 8-pound test on a medium to medium-light spinning rod with a pink and white Stingsilver. Other colors work well also; if the people next to you are catching fish and you aren't, see what kind of lures they are using.

If it's flounder you're after, you can find these flat fish in both Hatteras and Oregon inlets, in clear water. Anglers drift bottom rigs on medium-light spinning tackle. Croakers are found in the sounds around deep holes, oyster rocks and sloughs.

You can dine on almost all inshore species, but one bony fish with little food value that cannot be overlooked is the tarpon. A release category fish, the tarpon is probably one of the strongest fighting fish available inshore. While the Outer Banks is not a destination spot for tarpon, a handful of locals fish for them around Ocracoke in the Pamlico Sound and south to the mouth of the Neuse River. We recommend fresh-cut bait, such as spot or trout, and very sharp hooks to penetrate the tarpon's hard mouth. Remember, it's one thing to hook up and a whole other to bring a tarpon to the boat. Good luck!

Marinas

The Outer Banks is dotted with more than a half-dozen marinas that can help you book a charter for inshore or offshore fishing. You can call any of these marinas and request a particular captain or boat. If you are new in town, you'll be glad to know that the marinas book reputable captains on a rotating basis. While personalities vary, rarely does dependability.

If you want to ensure that you get to go fishing, especially during the busy holiday periods, it's wise to call at least a month in advance to make sure you get on board. The marinas stay open year round, so you can call well in advance of your trip if you know when you'll be vacationing here. Don't be afraid to ask questions (the marina personnel are very helpful), but if you wish to have a lengthy conversation, reservationists have more time to chat in the off-season.

Makeup parties are available for folks who want to hook up with a group to make six. If everything is booked up, ask to be put on a waiting list. The list below represents some of the choices in marinas on the Outer Banks. See our Watersports chapter for marina information for the individual boater.

Pirate's Cove Yacht Club
Nags Head/Manteo Cswy., Manteo • (252) 473-3906, (800) 367-4728

Salty Dawg Marina
U.S. Hwy. 64, Manteo • (252) 473-3405

Thicket Lump Marina
212 Thicket Lump Rd., Wanchese • (252) 473-4500

Oregon Inlet Fishing Center
N.C. Hwy. 12, Bodie Island • (252) 441-6301

Frisco Cove Marina
N.C. Hwy. 12, Frisco • (252) 995-4242

Hatteras Harbor Marina
N.C. Hwy. 12, Hatteras Village • (252) 986-2166, (800) 676-4939

Hatteras Landing Marina
N.C. Hwy. 12, Hatteras Village • (252) 986-2205, (800) 551-8478

Oden's Dock Marina
N.C. Hwy. 12, Hatteras Village • (252) 986-2555

Teach's Lair Marina
N.C. Hwy. 12, Hatteras Village • (252) 986-2460

Ocracoke Fishing Center and Anchorage Marina
N.C. Hwy. 12, Ocracoke Village • (252) 928-6661

Fishing the Backwaters

Journey the backwaters into a world of great beauty, peace and fish. Small boats fish Manns Harbor, the Alligator River or East and South lakes. There are several captains that offer backwater services. Check our list at the end of this section for more information.

You can troll, spin- and bait-cast or fly-fish year round on trips to our backwaters. You'll find an interesting mix of freshwater and saltwater species in the backwaters. Depending on the season, you can fish for crappie, rockfish (striped bass), largemouth bass, flounder, bream, sheepshead, drum, perch, croaker, spot, catfish and trout. How about that mix?!

The fishing is so laid-back that you might find the captain occasionally throwing in a line too. In these more protected waters, anglers can fish even when it's blowing offshore. If a storm comes, you can duck in behind an island. The most you can get is wet, and you're usually wading distance from shore.

Bring your camera. Depending on the time of day and season,

you might spot deer, bears and even alligators. It's a nice alternative to ocean fishing, and is a good choice for families.

Backwater Charters

If the following options are unavailable, you can always launch your own vessel from any of a number of local ramps (see our Watersports chapter) or contact the nearest marina or tackle shop for more information.

Phideaux Too
P.O. Box 343, Manns Harbor, NC 27953 • (252) 473-3059

Custom Sound Charters
152 Dogwood Tr., Manteo • (252) 473-1209

Fly-Fishing

Fly-fishing is a sport many Outer Banks anglers swear by, calling the fly-fishing opportunities here unlimited. You can fish the Pamlico, Croatan and Roanoke sounds for speckled trout, bluefish, puppy drum, little tunny, flounder and cobia.

Flat Out
P.O. Box 387, Nags Head, NC 27949 • (252) 449-0562

Captain Bryan De Hart's Coastal Adventures Guide Service
141 Brakewood Rd., Manteo • (252) 473-1575

Outer Banks Waterfowl
67 E. Dogwood Tr., Kitty Hawk • (252) 441-3732

Surf Fishing

Surf fishing is a popular Outer Banks pastime for the competitor or amateur alike. While there are miles of beach from which to cast a line, experienced local anglers say a surf-caster's success will vary depending on sloughs, temperature, currents and season. One of the hottest surf-casting spots on the Outer Banks is Cape Point, a sand spit at the tip of Cape Hatteras. Anglers often stand waist-deep in the churning waters, dutifully waiting for red drum to strike.

About nine months out of the year, anglers can fish for red drum on the Outer Banks. The best time to catch big drum is mid-October through mid-November. During this period large schools of drum are feeding on menhaden that migrate down the coastline. Cape Point is the hot spot for drum, but it tends to be a very crowded place to fish. A good second choice is the beach between Salvo and Buxton. But in the fall, you can capture them from Rodanthe down to Hatteras Inlet. From mid-April through about the third week in May, red drum show up around Ocracoke Inlet, both in the ocean and shallow shoal waters at the inlet's mouth and also in the Pamlico Sound.

Serious drum anglers fish after dark for the nocturnal feeders. Insiders prefer a southwesterly wind with an incoming tide and water temperatures in the low 60s. Big drum are known to come close to the surf during rough weather. Puppy drum or juvenile drum are easier to catch than the adult fish. They show in the surf after a northeast blow in late summer or early fall. Anglers use finger mullet with success as well as fresh shrimp (and we do mean fresh). Red drum are a regulated fish, both in size and limit. Call your local tackle shop for more information. If you're interested in learning more about red drum tag and release programs, call (252) 473-5734 or (252) 264-3911.

And speaking of Cape Point, the list of fish caught there is lengthy. Other common species include small, dogfish, Spanish mackerel, bluefish, pompano, striped bass and Spanish mackerel as well as bottom feeders such as croaker, flounder, spot, sea mullet and both gray and speckled trout. More uncommon are tarpon, cobia, amberjack, jack crevalles and shark weighing several hundred pounds.

Shoaling that takes place off Cape Hatteras makes Cape Point a haven for baitfish, and the influence of the nearby Gulf Stream and its warm-water jetties also contribute to the excellent fishing there. The beach accommodates many four-wheel-drive vehicles, and during peak season (spring and fall) is packed with anglers. If you want to try fishing Cape Point, take N.C. Highway 12 to Buxton and turn at the road that leads to the Cape Hatteras Lighthouse; it's well-marked by a sign. Turn right at the "T" in the road by the lighthouse, and then travel straight to the first vehicle access ramp, Ramp 43.

A section on surf fishing would not be complete without discussing bluefish. For years, we've enjoyed the arrival and subsequent blitzes of big bluefish during the Easter season and again around Thanksgiving. During a blitz, big blues chase baitfish up onto the beach in a feeding frenzy. This puts the blues in striking distance of ready surf-casters. It's a phenomenal sight to watch anglers reel in these fat and ferocious fish one after the other. Anglers line up along the shore like soldiers, and many a rod is bent in that telltale C-shape, fighting a bluefish. Some days you can see a sky full of birds feasting on the baitfish that the bluefish run toward the shore.

The last few years, the blues have not blitzed like they used to; however, 1997 did produce decent Thanksgiving weekend fishing for blues. As with most species, population figures (or at least landings) tend to rise and fall in cycles; perhaps they're tending toward a low point in the pattern. Maybe the big bluefin tuna, which feed on bluefish, are taking over these days, but blitz or not, you can usually catch some bluefish in the surf or in greater numbers offshore.

Pier Fishing

Pier fishing is a true Outer Banks institution and has delighted anglers young and old for more than 50 years. The appeal is obvious: low cost and a chance to fish deeper waters without a boat. The variety of fish available also lures anglers. Depending on the time of year, you can catch croakers, spot, sea mullet, red drum, cobia and occasionally a tarpon, king mackerel, sheepshead or amberjack.

Bait and tackle are sold at each pier, or you can rent whatever gear you need. Avid anglers usually come prepared, but newcomers to the sport are always welcome on the pier, and staff are more than willing to outfit you and offer some fishing tips. Pier fishing is a good way to introduce kids to the sport. Many Outer Banks locals spent their youth on the pier soaking in know-how and area fishing lore. For instance, Garry Oliver, who owns the Outer Banks Pier in South Nags Head, spent many a summer day at the Nags Head Fishing Pier when he was a lad. Today, Garry is a member of an award-winning surf-casters team.

Kitty Hawk Fishing Pier
N.C. Hwy. 12, MP 1, Kitty Hawk • (252) 261-2772

Avalon Fishing Pier
N.C. Hwy. 12, MP 6, Kill Devil Hills • (252) 441-7494

Nags Head Fishing Pier
N.C. Hwy. 12, MP 12, Nags Head • (252) 441-5141

Jennette's Pier
N.C. Hwy. 12, MP 16½, Nags Head • (252) 441-6116

Outer Banks Pier and Fishing Center
N.C. Hwy. 12, MP 18½, South Nags Head • (252) 441-5740

Hatteras Island Fishing Pier
N.C. Hwy. 12, Rodanthe • (252) 987-2323

Avon Golf & Fishing Pier
N.C. Hwy. 12, Avon • (252) 995-5480

Cape Hatteras Pier
N.C. Hwy. 12, Frisco • (252) 986-2533

Bait and Tackle Shops

Full-service tackle shops are scattered from Duck to Ocracoke. They are good sources for not only rods and reels, bait and other fishing gear but also for tips on what's biting and where. You'll find bait and tackle at all Outer Banks fishing piers and most marinas too. Just about every department store and general store on the islands carries some sort of fishing gear, and many shops also offer tackle rental. You can ask for guide information at any of the shops listed below.

Bob's Bait & Tackle
Duck Rd. and N.C. Hwy 12, Duck • (252) 261-8589

Kitty Hawk Bait & Tackle
U.S. Hwy. 158, MP 4½, Kitty Hawk • (252) 261-2955

TW's Bait & Tackle
U.S. Hwy. 158, MP 4, Kitty Hawk • (252) 261-7848

Whitney's Bait & Tackle
U.S. Hwy. 158, MP 4½, Kitty Hawk • (252) 261-5551

T.I.'s Bait & Tackle
U.S. Hwy. 158, MP 9, Kill Devil Hills • (252) 441-3166

Tatem's Tackle Box Inc.
U.S. Hwy. 158, MP 13, Nags Head • (252) 441-7346

Capt. Marty's Fishing and Hunting Tackle Shop
U.S. Hwy. 158, MP 14, Nags Head • (252) 441-3132

Whalebone Tackle
U.S. Hwy. 158 at U.S. Hwy. 64 Jct., Whalebone Junction • (252) 441-7413

Fishing Unlimited
Nags Head/Manteo Cswy., U.S. Hwy. 64 • (252) 441-5028

The Fishin' Hole
27202 Sand St., Salvo • (252) 987-2351

Frank and Fran's Fisherman's Friend
N.C. Hwy. 12, Avon • (252) 995-4171

Cape Point Tackle
N.C. Hwy. 12, Buxton • (252) 995-3147

Dillon's Corner
N.C. Hwy. 12, Buxton • (252) 995-5083

Red Drum Tackle Shop
N.C. Hwy. 12, Buxton • (252) 995-5414

Frisco Rod and Gun
N.C. Hwy. 12, Frisco • (252) 995-5366

Tradewinds
N.C. Hwy. 12, Ocracoke • (252) 928-5491

O'Neal's Dockside Tackle Shop
N.C. Hwy. 12, Ocracoke • (252) 928-1111

Fishing Reports

For the latest word on what's biting, check with the following sources:

Kitty Hawk Fishing Pier
(252) 261-2772

Nags Head Fishing Pier
(252) 441-5141

Pirate's Cove Yacht Club
(252) 473-3906

Oregon Inlet Fishing Center
(252) 441-6301

Red Drum Tackle Shop
(252) 995-5414

Frisco Pier
(252) 986-2533

Hatteras Island Fishing Pier
(252) 987-2323

O'Neal's Dockside
(252) 928-1111

Also read *The Virginian-Pilot* daily North Carolina section and *The Carolina Coast* for Damon Tatem's report. Check out Joe Malat's informative column in the weekly *Outer Banks Sentinel*. For more Insiders' information, you can pick up a copy of the *Sportfishing Report*, the Outer Banks first fishing magazine, which has now expanded to cover the entire East Coast. This magazine is available on the newsstands or by calling (252) 480-3133. Subscriptions are available.

Index of Advertisers

Index

Index

Index

Index